D1301477

REAL MONEY ANSWERS®
FOR MEN

The Ultimate Playbook for Financial Success

By
THE WISDOM & WEALTH MONEY MAVEN
PATRICE C. WASHINGTON

Seek Wisdom Find Wealth
Atlanta   Los Angeles

Real Money Answers for Men

www.PatriceWashington.com

ISBN # 978-0-9859080-3-4

Published by Seek Wisdom Find Wealth, Mableton, GA 30126

Printed in the United States of America

First Printing, August 2014

Photography by Chad Finley

Cover Design by dw3design.net

Layout Design by JERA Publishing, Roswell, GA

Writing Credit to Candice L. Davis, Atlanta, GA

**This book is available at quantity discounts for bulk purchases.
For information, please call 404-913-4479.**

To my husband, Gerald, You have definitely taught me a lot about the money game and financial success. From successful businesses to scraping up change together to feed Reagan, your unwavering strength, love, leadership, partnership and dedication made the once uncomfortable not only comfortable, but now safe and enjoyable. I couldn't imagine sharing these financial blessings or blunders with anyone else. I love you.

To the many men around the world who have allowed me to become your Money Maven too, I thank you. I wrote this book for you and pray that you are blessed by the wisdom within.

Special thanks to the men who took time each week to answer my questions about men and money. I couldn't have completed Real Money Answers for Men without you!

Anthony Davis

Chike Uzoka

Clayton Davis

Gerald Martin

Jeremiah Ojo

Keyshawn Johnson

Michael Matthews

Michael Neyland

Sean Connor

Terrance Crockett

Vern Ross

CONTENTS

WHY I WROTE THIS BOOK

NO QUARTERBACK WOULD GO into a game without studying his playbook, assessing his strengths and weaknesses, and watching plenty of film of the opposing team. He wants to have every possible strategy at his disposal and know what to expect from the other team so he can have the absolute best chance to win the game. I wrote this book as your financial playbook, with specific steps you can use to manage your money to reach your financial goals. In these pages, I also show you how to identify and avoid or overcome any money obstacles that might prevent you from finally winning with money.

The average American man has over $26,000 in consumer debt, and that's before we factor in mortgages. When asked how much money they had in savings, 61% of men said they *don't* have enough money saved to cover three months of living expenses. The media tends to focus on the income and career path disparities between men and women, but it's clear that most men aren't winning with money either. More and more, men are tweeting, emailing, and hitting me up on Facebook for advice on how to step up their money game. They're hungry for a resource that can answer all their questions.

I've already written a comprehensive book on personal finance, and every day, more readers are implementing the principles in that book and taking charge of their money. There's just one problem. Not many men want to walk around carrying a bright pink paperback with the title *Real Money Answers for Every Woman.*

After talking with some of the men in my classes and workshops, it became clear that slapping a blue cover on the original material wouldn't be enough. Good information is good information, but men have different financial expectations and responsibilities they try to live up to, and they often face a different set of money challenges from the ones women encounter. I wanted to address all of that and write a book that spoke directly to the male money experience.

One of the most significant differences between men and women in the area of money is that men have to deal with the myth that they should already know everything about personal finance just because they were born male. That misguided belief often keeps them from seeking information or asking questions, even though it's ridiculous to expect anyone to come out of the womb knowing how to make and manage money. Fortunately, more and more men are rejecting that myth. They're tired of pretending to have it all under control when no one ever taught them how to budget, pay off debt, or increase their income. They're reaching out to whatever resources they can find to get clarity on how to make more of their money.

While I've taught men in the past, I decided to challenge myself to dig deeper and really understand their needs in the area of personal finance before writing this book. As the number of men in my audience grows, I want to make sure I serve them as well as I serve their wives, sisters, and mothers. I invited a group of men to discuss money with me in a private Facebook group, and they generously responded. I used their questions and concerns to create the material you'll find in these pages.

If you're comfortable with your level of financial success, that's great. You'll still find information here to take you even further. If like most people, however, you're struggling in some area of your finances, this book will help you take control. It doesn't matter if you earn less than most of your friends, if you've racked up thousands in debt, or if you've faced foreclosure or filed bankruptcy. As I like to say, "So what? Now What?" What's done is done, but if you open your mind to the information in this book and make the decision to take action, you can get your financial life in order. Don't wait any longer. The sooner you make a change, the better. I don't want you to end up like the gentleman who recently emailed me hoping to schedule some time to talk about how to fix his finances. "I'm about to retire," he wrote, "and I don't have anything to show for all my years of work." What a difference it would've made for him if he'd had this information in his thirties or forties.

Unlike so many people, you won't be able to plead ignorance. You'll have no excuse for reaching retirement with little to show for your decades of labor. Every fundamental principle you need to know to avoid ending up in those circumstances is in this book. If you're a beginner in the world of personal finance, don't worry. I've covered all the basics. And if you think you already have a pretty good handle on your money, my job is to build on what you know and make sure you *master* the subject.

MY MONEY STORY

N 2003, I GRADUATED from college with $18,000 in credit card debt— despite the fact that I received more than enough grants, scholarships, student loans, and parental assistance throughout my collegiate career. I even worked a full-time job the entire time I was a student, so it wasn't like I relied on the credit cards to buy textbooks or to get cash advances to pay my rent. I didn't spend money on designer purses or take extravagant spring break trips either.

So how did I manage to run up my credit card bills so quickly? Over the course of four years, I made one poor spending choice after another. Those small decisions snowballed until I was in way over my head. Once I realized what I'd done, I got busy doing the hard work of getting my finances in order, and along the way I discovered that my financial journey hadn't begun with that first credit card in college. It started way back when I was a six-year-old carrying my mother's expired credit cards in my Betty Boop purse. I had to unpack all of what I'd learned about money growing up to understand how to manage my money as an adult.

I committed myself to paying off that debt and getting my personal finances in order, and at the same time, I built a successful seven-figure real estate, mortgage, and escrow business. Unfortunately, the recession hit, the bottom fell out of the housing market, and I lost it all. With savings exhausted and bills piling up, I took on jobs for which I was completely overqualified just to make ends meet.

But I worked my way back. I built a new business, Seek Wisdom Find Wealth, with a stronger foundation. I took the lessons I learned from my financial ups and downs and used them to help thousands of people through personal finance coaching, workshops, speaking engagements, articles, and books. *Real Money Answers for Men* is a continuation of my efforts to teach anyone willing to learn how to win with money.

HOW TO USE THIS BOOK

KEEP AN OPEN MIND, and trust the process I've laid out, even when you don't quite understand why I ask you to do something. Whatever your starting point, I suggest you read this book from beginning to end. You may think you already know enough about a certain subject area, but do yourself a favor and read through it anyway. You might discover one little nugget that will make a difference in your financial life. As you read, please also apply the strategies. I've learned that information without implementation is just plain useless, and I want this book to be a catalyst for deep transformation in your money journey.

I highly suggest you keep a journal as a companion to this book. Use it to answer the questions you'll find in each chapter and to note your plans for change. Before you conjure up images of a sweet little diary with a gold lock on it, let me tell you, real men do keep journals—including my husband. Recently, Gerald journaled about an upcoming business transaction. He recorded the outcome he wanted to get and how the deal would go in his ideal world. Writing it down helped him to strategize and to release any anxiety about the conversations he needed to have. Looking back a few months later, he realized the deal had gone just as he'd written it out. He hadn't discussed the specifics with anyone, but the major players who got on board, the funding, and the profit turned out exactly as he'd written about them. There's power in putting your ideas in writing. By keeping a journal, you're creating a custom playbook for your life and your unique financial circumstances.

Finally, come back to this book as a reference when you're dealing with specific money issues. Reading through it one time probably won't be enough for permanent, positive change.

For those of you in committed relationships, it's a good idea for your wife or girlfriend to read *Real Money Answers for Every Woman* at the same time. Money fights and lack of communication about finances are the leading cause of divorce. It can make such a difference to your relationship when the two of you are in agreement about earning, spending, saving, and investing.

If you're ready to take your money mindset and skill set to the next level, or if you want support and answers to your specific questions on your personal finance journey, I invite you to check out my Mindset + Money Master Class and join the hundreds of people who've used the course to experience financial breakthroughs. I'll be there to help.

Patrice

P.S. I have to give credit to my husband, Gerald, for all the sports analogies, references, and examples. Without his input, you might be reading about stilettos and designer bags!

LOOK FOR THESE HELPFUL NOTES THROUGHOUT

Real TALK	Real MONEY	UN REAL	AFFIRM
Quotes and expressions to remember	Savings tips or financial illustrations	Statistics or stories that need to stick	Positive declarations to repeat and remember

CREATE WEALTHY HABITS

"Excellence is not a singular act but a habit. You are what you do repeatedly."
- Shaquille O'Neal

REAL MONEY ANSWERS FOR MEN was written as a quick, practical, playbook with real answers to some of your most pressing money questions. This section, *Create Wealthy Habits*, will give you what I consider to be the absolute foundation of personal finance success. It's about teaching you the basic principle that any successful person will share with you: True success starts on the inside; the outside is merely the byproduct.

We are creatures of habit. Period. Most people understand this on the surface. The part they don't get, however, is that habits come in two forms: habits of doing and habits of not doing. You probably recognize the things you actively do each day as habits, good or bad. But when you fail to do what you should be doing, the not doing becomes your habit. When it comes to your money, not doing can leave you broke and wondering how you ended up that way.

Boxing champion Mike Tyson reportedly earned more than $400 million over his career, but his thinking and beliefs about money kept him from holding onto that fortune. In 2003, he

Real TALK

You're either doing or you're not doing. There is no in-between.

filed for bankruptcy, claiming a debt load of $27 million. His non-wealthy habits—overspending, taking on too much debt, failing to pay taxes—were so ingrained in him that hundreds of millions of dollars couldn't keep him afloat. Clearly, he also had a habit of not doing things like budgeting, saving, and investing.

If you aren't practicing wealthy habits, then you're more than likely practicing non-wealthy habits, just like "Iron Mike" was. The two go hand in hand. Once you acknowledge that and begin to take action to change the way you think about money and improve your wealthy habits, you can move onward and upward. The choice is ultimately yours. The information you need is right here. Get ready to learn the stuff you didn't even know you needed to know. Get ready to create, and more importantly, implement wealthy habits!

MONEY MINDSETS, ATTITUDES & MYTHS

Building wealth has 100% nothing to do with money; it has 100% everything to do with you and your mindset towards money.

WHEN A QUARTERBACK SEES that a play isn't going to work, he can call an audible and change the plan midway through. You may have made some bad money choices so far, but you too can change your play midway through. You don't have to stick with what you've been doing, especially if what you've been doing doesn't work. It all starts with changing your mindset about money.

Listen up and pay very close attention here. Contrary to popular belief, financial success isn't really about money at all. It's about recognizing where these beliefs were formed and reconditioning them to support the life you desire, deserve, and have declared you will work diligently to bring forth.

We all have those lies, large and small, that we tell ourselves to justify why we do the things we do. The reality is, however, that every single decision you make is either helping you or hurting you. There really isn't much grey area there. Whether or not you choose to acknowledge it now really doesn't matter. Your long-term financial standing will inevitably show you what you deemed important during your short-term decision-making.

There is absolutely no coincidence that you have this book in your hands. It's time to uncover the lies—I mean, mindsets, attitudes, and myths—that have been holding you back from financial freedom.

REAL MEN NATURALLY KNOW HOW TO HANDLE MONEY.

I actually believe that real men know how to acknowledge their weaknesses just as much as their strengths. And even further, they know how to communicate when they need help. Money management is learned behavior. No one is born with the skills and knowledge to manage money well. Don't beat yourself up because you were never taught what to do with your money. At the end of the day, we all need to learn the basic life skills of how to budget, earn more money, save, and invest. If you don't know enough yet, now is the time to learn more about how to make the most of your money. You have nothing to hide, nothing to defend, nothing to protect, and no reason to pretend. On the contrary, you have everything in the world to gain.

A MAN SHOULD ALWAYS EARN MORE THAN HIS WIFE.

Earning less money than your wife or girlfriend does not make you less of a man. As a society, we've created an expectation that a man will always be the primary breadwinner, and this assumption puts unfair pressure on many men. Every relationship is different, but a woman who loves you won't try to make you feel inferior because your salary is lower than hers. Be confident in who you are and what you bring to the relationship.

A COUPLE BUCKS NEVER HURT ANYONE.

Millionaires keep up with every penny, and you should too.

Speak for yourself. I heard someone say once that the dollar menu is the quickest way to go broke. Small charges add up and can eventually break the budget and the bank. Paying $34 overdraft fees for a quick $5 swipe at the gas station or a $1 water bottle makes no sense. Millionaires watch the bottom line and keep up with every penny, so I suggest you start sweating the small stuff, sir. It's important that you get in the habit of asking yourself, "Do I *really* need this?" or "Can I find this somewhere else for less?" even with purchases that seem like no big deal.

IF I MADE MORE MONEY, THIS WOULD BE EASIER.

Just stop. It absolutely would not. Without discipline, you could double your income and still have tons of debt and no savings. Hell, you could triple it this year and be worse off than you are today in less than three years. How do I know this? Look at all the entertainers, athletes, and—my favorite—lottery winners, who end up flat broke and in deep debt despite having access to millions. Don't assume that more money is the answer. If you refuse to dig deep and get serious about managing $100, then having $100,000, whether you won it or earned it, won't all of a sudden make you better with money. I know it's hard to believe, but just trust me on this one.

I'LL START LATER.

This is one of the ultimate myths. I love it when a client tries to tell me he plans to get on his money game, but he just needs to get through some important event first. After the holiday season, after he starts the new job, after the wedding he has to pay for, after whatever. In case you can't relate yet, let me tell you what the typical excuses—I mean "rational reasons"—sound like and what the people who hear them are probably thinking.

Oh, it's at the top of my New Year's resolution list!
Awesome, but it's June. Six months? Really?

I'll start paying off debt after the holidays.
Of course. You need time to pile on some more debt first, right?

Once I get my income tax refund next year, I'll pay everything.
Yeah, so no discipline implemented there. With no strategy and no savings plan, you'll be back in debt by June.

Get the point? I hope so, because here's the problem with continuing to delay things. Something more important or necessary will always be going on or coming up in your life.

So what are you *really* waiting for? It's easy to *talk* about change, but when will you take action and just start already? If you don't start today, years may go by, and whatever you're waiting on may never come.

I DON'T MAKE ENOUGH TO SAVE.

Ouch! I've been bitten by this one before. One of the lines I used to tell myself and hear all the time is, "I can't afford to save, pay down debt, blah, blah, blah." I'll tell you what I tell them. You can't afford not to save!

I recently sat down with an advisor friend from one of the country's largest financial firms. He told me that his most successful clients all have one thing in common: they're disciplined about their savings and clear about their values and goals. He shared candidly that some of the families with the best portfolios are those that have earned less than $80,000 per year, but have been saving and investing for decades.

The very folks who believe they can't save somehow manage to give the bank $34 per overdraft fee each month or $29 for late credit card payments. If you can involuntarily pay the bank money every month, there should be a way to voluntarily squeeze out a few bucks to fund your savings account. If it's the best you can do right now, start putting just an extra $10 towards paying off your debt. You have to start somewhere, and you have to start *today*.

Real TALK

When it comes to saving, you have to start somewhere, and you have to start today.

I DON'T KNOW ANYTHING ABOUT MONEY.

I'm sorry. Is that supposed to fly with search engines like Google at your fingertips? You don't have to be an "expert" to know that if you spend less than you earn, save money, invest money, and plan for the future, you'll be better off. This timeless wisdom has been passed on for generations by ancestors who didn't have access to the education you've enjoyed.

Isn't it worth the time spent doing a little extra research to get rid of harassing phone calls, have money saved, and have greater options in case of an emergency? There are far too many personal finance books, blogs, professional coaches, and non-profit counseling agencies offering complimentary classes on credit and money management for you to remain in the dark. Find a few resources that work for you, and just stick with it.

IT'S GOOD DEBT.

Where did this ridiculous rumor originate? Despite what you've heard, student loans and mortgages are *not* good debt. There's no such thing. The best debt is the debt you don't owe anymore! If you're only keeping your mortgage for the tax write-off, try this: give more to your

The only good debt, is debt you don't owe anymore.

place of worship or favorite charity. You can write that off, without all the wasted interest payments.

Are there times in life when you'll need to leverage debt to get ahead? Of course. But when you classify something as "good," there's no intention or intensity behind your desire to get rid of it.

When you understand that repaying someone considerably more than you borrowed is a waste of your hard earned money, you can get serious about a plan to pay off the debt.

I hope a few of these mindsets, attitudes, and myths have struck a chord. Now that you know the thoughts and beliefs that have been misguiding you and stopping you from winning with money the way you want to, it's time to learn how to change them. The sooner you tell yourself the truth, the sooner you'll be able to take charge and change your financial life once and for all!

The sooner you tell yourself the truth, the sooner you can change your financial life.

WEALTH BEGINS WITHIN

THE BACK OF MY business cards used to read: *Changing roots, changing fruits, changing lives.* Roots are the things deep down inside you that cause you to act and think a certain way. Fruits are the results those thoughts and actions produce in your life. Your bank account balance, where you live, the opportunities that come your way, and the relationships you currently have are all the fruits of your own thinking and choices.

A lot of people falsely assume that if they switch banks, or move to a new city, or dump the person they're dating, everything in their lives, including their personal finances, will improve. But more often than not, the same old behaviors sneak back in, even in a new environment or with a new person. You end up with the same fruits. Until you change your roots, you will never change your fruits, and you will never change your life.

Think of it this way. If you reap what you sow, can you really keep planting apple seeds and expecting oranges? Can you really keep tally of your expenses in your head and expect to not overdraft? Can you really continue to not save money and act surprised when your emergencies become drama-filled catastrophes? Can you really continue to buy your children everything under the sun and expect them to respect money?

This is more than learning how to write a budget or balance a checkbook. It's not about starting a business or earning a promotion. The desire and discipline to do all of those things consistently and successfully must come from something inside you. It starts with your thoughts, values, beliefs, and mindset. Your road to wealth begins within.

WHAT THE HECK IS A FINANCIAL BLUEPRINT, ANYWAY?

No one is born with a particular attitude toward money. You were taught, just like we all were, how to think about and handle money matters. These subconscious beliefs, ideas, thoughts, and actions are what create your financial blueprint.

In addition to your parents, your money influences could include siblings, friends, teachers, and religious doctrine or leaders you were exposed to during adolescence. Unless they're first recognized and then reconditioned, it's very likely that the lessons and habits you learned as a child will continue to cause you to subconsciously sabotage your own success with money.

To determine your financial blueprint, consider the following factors.

VERBAL INFLUENCES: What did you hear about money, wealth, and rich people when you were growing up? Did you hear things like *filthy rich, money can't buy love, the poor are closer to God, money is the root of all evil, it takes money to make money,* or *you only need enough to get by?*

MODELING: What did you witness in regards to how your parents obtained, managed, and allocated money? Did they have any systems or budgets in place? Was money a source of joy or stress for your family? Did your parents argue about money often or sit down and plan together?

SPECIFIC INCIDENTS: What experiences do you remember about money, wealth, and rich people? Were you ever embarrassed at a cash register because a credit card was declined? Did you experience eviction notices or interrupted utility services? Ever been teased for not having the latest clothing or electronic gadget?

After taking a moment to record your initial thoughts, give yourself additional time to reflect. Carefully consider each of these categories and complete the following exercise for each influence.

AWARENESS: Reflect upon the things that were said, the behaviors you witnessed, and a specific incident you experienced in regards to money and wealth. Not everyone endures negative experiences. Some people even have feelings of financial guilt for not having grown up in difficult financial circumstances. Write down how your life today may be similar to or different from each of the things you remember.

UNDERSTANDING: Describe the effects these words, habits, and incidents from your youth have had on your financial life.

DISASSOCIATION: Separate who you are today from what you witnessed as a child. Your parents chose that life, and you have a choice in the present moment to be different. How will you choose to break this cycle in your family? What steps can you take to be a better example and influence for the young people around you?

MY PARENTS DIDN'T TEACH ME ANYTHING ABOUT MONEY. NOW WHAT?

ANSWER #1: Welcome to the club.

ANSWER #2: Accept it and move on.

The bottom line is everyone has something they can legitimately blame their parents for doing, or not doing, which negatively impacted them. At some point, however, you have to be an adult and let it go to truly to move on with your own life. Becoming wealthy, getting out of debt, saving, investing, and the like won't happen until you take ownership of your life. Let's face it. The blame game is not sexy and most importantly, it's not productive. It's not a trait of a wealthy man on the road to accomplishing his dreams.

Remember, your parents are someone's children, too. They may have learned their poor financial habits from your beloved Gram and Pops. (See: *What the heck is a financial blueprint, anyway?*) Just be happy you have a chance to break that generational cycle. All you can do now is make sure you do your part to expose your family to a totally different mindset and blueprint towards money and wealth-building principles.

It doesn't matter how old you are. If you're still alive, then you've still got time to correct the wrongs of your childhood!

HOW DO I START CHANGING THE WAY
I THINK ABOUT MONEY?

This is no easy task, especially if you grew up hearing, seeing, and forming a lot of negative money and wealth-creation habits. (See: *What the heck is a financial blueprint, anyway?*) But a part of being wealthy is having the mindset that money is an important tool that, when utilized properly, helps you create the life you want. When used improperly it can become a source of anxiety, stress, and strife.

Money is an important tool that can help me create the life I want.

The difference between non-wealthy people and wealthy people is simply the way they think about money. The only way to progress and move past your past is to replace your previous thinking with a new and fresh perspective, and I believe wholeheartedly in using positive affirmations as one tool to do so. Below are a few samples of what I used to change my thinking.

When I first began my journey, I created simple statements I could recite in the shower or while I was driving to the office each day.

Old Way of Thinking:	*I'm clueless about money. I don't even know where to start.*
New Way of Thinking:	I am ready, willing, and able to manage my money!
Old Way of Thinking:	*It's just a penny. That's nothing.*
New Way of Thinking:	The cents matter just as much as the dollars do! I love ALL money!
Old Way of Thinking:	*Money is so hard to come by.*
New Way of Thinking:	Money flows to me easily, freely, and often!
Old Way of Thinking:	*I work hard, so I deserve it.*
New Way of Thinking:	I deserve to be wealthy because of the value I add to others.

Old Way of Thinking:	*I'm just that person everyone depends on.*
New Way of Thinking:	I empower the people I love to take responsibility for their own finances.

If you're on my mailing list, you know that each week I send out original Wisdom & Wealth Affirmations and personal reflection exercises to help you grow your mind and your money. While I love my one-liners, I also share longer affirming statements, so that readers can get clear about the full context of what they're declaring over their lives. Below is a sample of one of my favorites.

I AM the CEO of my life.

I set the strategy, goals, and vision for my life. **I own my successes. I own my failures. I understand that success is going from failure to failure without loss of enthusiasm.** When I experience a major challenge, I reinvent myself in the marketplace. I protect my brand at all costs. Quality control is in my hands. **I choose team players that work to fulfill the mission and vision**. I fire those who do not get the job done. I focus only on the activities which produce positive returns. I take 100% responsibility for the outcomes in my life.

I AM the CEO of my life.

Powerful stuff, right?

Now let's go a step beyond just thinking these types of thoughts. What do you think could happen if instead of focusing on and complaining about the things you don't want, you spoke these positive things over your life? Remember, what you verbalize you magnify and magnetize in your own life.

Visit www.RealMoneyAnswers.com to register for my weekly newsletter which features these Wisdom & Wealth Affirmations to help keep you on track with growing your mind and money.

WHAT CAN I DO TO CREATE WEALTHIER HABITS?

I have to reiterate that most people understand the idea that we humans are "creatures of habit." The part they don't get, however, is that when you don't do anything to change negative habits, then you create a habit of not doing. I spend a lot of time, actually more time than I care to admit, asking people to stop telling me what they're *trying* to do. You're either doing or you're not doing. There's no wiggle room here, gentlemen. Either you have doing habits or not-doing habits. For example, reading is one thing, but being in the habit of implementing what you read is a completely different story. Knowledge doesn't create success. Action creates success. So make sure you act on the following eight points. Specific ways to do so are found throughout the book.

Real TALK

Knowledge doesn't create success. Action creates success.

1. GET CLEAR ABOUT YOUR GOALS

It's impossible to get what you want if you aren't exactly sure of what that is. Habakkuk 2:2 tells us, "Write down your vision and make it plain." You need to be clear about your intentions in order to bring them forth. You must write them down and be as concrete as possible with any details, especially those dealing with numbers or financial objectives. My mentor, media mogul Steve Harvey, often tells the story of the day he sat in his elementary school classroom and wrote on a piece of paper his expectation that he would one day appear on television. His teacher told him he was being unrealistic. The idea that a little boy she taught might grow up to do something so ambitious seemed absurd to her. But Steve Harvey saved that note and read it to himself every day for over thirty years. Today, no matter what time you flip on the television, you can probably catch him hosting *Family Feud*, chatting with guests on the Emmy award-winning daytime talk show bearing his name, or making people laugh on repeats of the syndicated sitcom, *The Steve Harvey Show*. See where I'm going here?

You'll be amazed at how opportunities show up to lead you in the direction of your goal. (For complete steps on financial goal-setting, see: *How do I set financial goals I can achieve?*)

2. DECLARE A PURPOSE

You have to know the *why* behind what you want. Without declaring a purpose, you'll continue to live in the moment and blindly throw away money, or even worse, lie to yourself about why you're not closer to where you'd like to be. (See: *Money Mindsets, Attitudes & Myths.*) Knowing the *why* of what you're doing will keep you focused on reaching both long-term and short-term goals. Your purpose helps you prioritize your actions and invest in activities that push you closer to what you say you want.

3. COMMIT TO A LIFESTYLE OF LEARNING

Education doesn't stop after the diploma or the degree. Did you know the difference between where you are today and where you'll be in five years is directly related to the people you associate with and the books you read? In *How Rich People Think*, Steve Siebold shares a very sad, yet true observation. "Walk into a wealthy person's home and one of the first things you'll see is an extensive library of books they've used to educate themselves on how to become more successful," he writes. "The middle class reads novels, tabloids and entertainment magazines."

Wealthy people commit to a lifestyle of education, and non-wealthy people commit to a lifestyle of simply being entertained. Even if you don't categorize yourself as a reader, it's time to find the mode of learning that works for you. You can attend seminars and conferences, dial into teleconferences, log on to webinars, or invest in

Real TALK

Wealthy people commit to a lifestyle of learning, not a lifestyle of entertainment.

coaching or finding a mentor or mastermind group. Figure out what works for you, but commit from this day forward to never stop learning.

4. UNDERSTAND YOUR VALUE

Understanding your value allows you to create wealth in two ways. First, you learn how to respond to people or situations that threaten your financial success. When you don't understand your value, your own self-worth, you're at risk of associating money with different thoughts and actions that don't support your long-term vision. You allow yourself to be taken advantage of by mooching family members, because you falsely believe you're giving and/or receiving love or some other desired emotion.

Second, understanding your value helps you know what to charge for your service or products. You're blessed with unique abilities, gifts, skills, and talents, just as every person is. Selling yourself short is an insult to God. He gives us the ability to produce wealth, but when we don't maximize that potential to the fullest, we can't turn around and beg God for more financially. Once you understand and declare your value, you'll be much more comfortable having difficult conversations with loved ones or charging what you're worth and communicating that to potential clientele.

5. GET VISUAL

Any new invention starts as an image in the inventor's mind. In 1903, when the first airplane was created, Orville and Wilbur Wright had only a mental image of what this flying machine would become. Until they put this image on paper and created a sketch and a blueprint, it was nothing more than a dream. Reaching your personal finance goals cannot continue to simply be a dream. You need a blueprint. You need a visual representation of your financial goals.

I've always used picture journals and dream boards to help me bring my imagination into reality. You can do the same. Find magazine photos or pictures online and post them where you'll see them every day. Use the power of your visual sense to keep you focused on your goal. This focus is what will keep you motivated over the long haul.

6. MAINTAIN A GRATEFUL SPIRIT

AFFIRM

I possess all of my needs, as well as my wants.

Once again, what you verbalize you magnify and magnetize in your life. When you dwell on the negative aspects of your life, you repel financial success, and any other type of success. When you remain grateful for those things, no matter how few, which are going right in your life, you find wealth in whatever situation you may be experiencing at any given moment. When you're grateful for what you already have, as well as those things you desire, you become happier and healthier and can attract more of the same.

7. DEVELOP A "SO WHAT? NOW WHAT?" ATTITUDE

The reality is that obstacles are going to be thrown your way, no matter how much positive thinking and prayer you use. Instead of allowing life's distractions to knock you off course, accept them, learn the lessons, and move on, continuously pressing toward your goals. When you look life head-on and say, "This challenge happened, but what can I do now to move on?" you'll reach goals you never thought were possible. Adopting this attitude teaches you to act in spite of your own doubts and fears or ridicule from others. When you press on despite the unexpected, you build the courage to take down challenges one by one! When you press on in the face of obstacles, you strengthen your ability to handle future challenges.

Real TALK

When you press on in the face of obstacles, you strengthen your ability to take on future challenges.

8. GIVE WELL, RECEIVE WELL

Believe it or not, many of us aren't good at giving or receiving. You may think you are, but if you really study your habits in everyday things, you may be shocked at what you discover.

You may feel like a great giver when you help a relative, but when was the last time you gave to an absolute stranger? You might be quick to walk another offering to the altar at your church where people know you, but when's the last time you picked a charity to support because you really believed in the good work the organization does? Truly good givers give to uplift and champion others, even when no one is looking.

Are you able to ask for help when you need it, without feeling embarrassed or ashamed? Perhaps you feel uncomfortable when someone offers you a hand. People who receive well can ask for help and receive it with appreciation, not guilt.

The bottom line is giving and receiving work in perfect harmony. You must give in order to receive, and the more you receive, the more you are expected to give again. Have you noticed how philanthropic the world's wealthiest people are? As much as you hear about their giving, you don't see Oprah or Bill Gates running out of money.

WHERE DO I FIND THE MOTIVATION TO CHANGE MY HABITS?

I was blown away the first time someone asked me this question. I had never really thought about it, and honestly, I still can't say I have a definitive response. This is one of those questions that could have a different answer from one person to the next.

I've found that, like me, my clients are usually motivated by the past, the future, or a hybrid of the two. I didn't grow up in the best neighborhood. I lived with my mother and grandmother above a storefront on a main street in South Central Los Angeles. I've heard and seen drive-by shootings firsthand, and I've witnessed people shooting up drugs in the alley behind my building. When I was very young, these things, along with other experiences I won't share here, motivated me to work hard, go to college, and declare that I was *not* coming back.

Now that I'm a mother myself, a huge part of my motivation is making sure my children never have to experience the negative elements or difficult environments I did. I'm also motivated by the fact that I enjoy a certain lifestyle and would prefer to hang on to it until I exit life stage left. I've been there, done that with the harassing phone calls from creditors, the money wasted on overdraft fees, and the arguments with people about finances. Frankly, I've reached a point of being sick and tired of being sick and tired, and I really could do without going back to that place.

Look to your past, present, and future and to the people that matter most to you to find the motivation to change your habits.

WITH MY TRACK RECORD, AM I REALLY CAPABLE OF IMPROVING MY FINANCIAL SITUATION?

Because of past financial failures, many men feel inadequate when it comes to handling money. Feeling like you may not have what it takes to be a good provider is a heavy burden to carry. But there's no reason to feel inadequate when it comes to handling your money. Anyone can acquire basic personal finance skills. The change won't happen overnight because, after all, the results you have today took some time to materialize. But with consistent work, it can and will happen. Take a stand and decide to do things differently, starting now.

If your self-doubt in this area seems too hard to overcome, there are solutions available to you. Financial therapy for individuals, couples, and families who desire to understand the emotional triggers and experiences that cause them to struggle with finances and

AFFIRM

I view every limitation as a new possibility.

make poor financial decisions is a relatively new and growing field. (Yes, real men get help when they need it!) It can help you communicate better about money, uncover irrational financial beliefs, and move forward with your financial plans. If your need goes further than the scope of this book, don't hesitate to check out a financial therapist in your area. Visit www.financialtherapyassociation.org.

SETTING THE FOUNDATION

THE LAST TIME YOU decided to get your finances in order, where did you start? With a copy of your credit report or a freshly printed budget from Microsoft Excel templates? When most people start working on their finances, they kick things off with these sorts of external activities and completely ignore any internal factors. They soon find all this action is only busywork. Their motivation fizzles out because there's no foundation sustaining it.

Building a successful foundation with finances begins on the inside, not the outside. It's not so much about your budgeting skills as it is about your beliefs concerning money. Personal finance guru Barbara Stanny put it best when she broke down the three core levels on which financial success is based.

The first level is the Inner Work of Wealth, which deals with your mindset. This means understanding your fears, beliefs, and attitudes surrounding money, wealth, and financial success, as well as understanding where they originated. This gets to the root of how you feel about money.

Some people assume that we all *love* money, but many of us have a totally different relationship with it. Every change in life must begin with a decision, and until you can recognize the *what* and *where* of your relationship with money, you'll never really make the decision to implement the steps necessary to recondition yourself.

The second level is the Outer Work of Wealth, which deals with developing money-managing skills. This covers earning money, understanding your worth and charging appropriately for it—whether you choose to work in your own business or in someone else's—and the way you save, spend, and invest. Understanding your natural inclination in these activities is a part of discovering your personal money style, which is key to laying the foundation for your success.

Real TALK

Until you understand your money mindset, you'll never be able to change your relationship with money.

The third and final level is the Higher Work of Wealth. This is where we obtain our sense of giving and helping others. It also dictates our relationships and conversations that involve money.

If you were to see it as a hierarchy, the Higher Work is at the top, and it's easiest to do when a strong foundation has been laid—in terms of the proper money mindset and skill set—to sustain it.

WHAT IS PERSONAL FINANCE, REALLY?

Personal finance deals with your individual relationship with money. It serves as your financial outline, addressing the ways you obtain, budget, save, spend, and manage monetary resources. These behaviors can change at various stages throughout your lifetime, taking into account a mixture of external financial variables, like home value depreciations or stock market declines, and major life events, like getting your first job or getting married.

Some of the major components of personal finance include checking and savings accounts, credit cards, consumer and student loans, invest-

✔AFFIRM

I am ready, willing, and able to manage my money wisely and successfully!

ment principles, income taxes, and much more, depending on which phase of life you're in. A positive relationship with money forces you to continuously assess your responses to important questions.

These questions are the foundation for creating a personal financial plan:

How much money and how many financial assets do I possess today?
How much money will I need at various points in the future?
How do I go about getting that money in the present?

The most basic plan will always include these five steps:

1. Assessment: *Where are you now?*

2. Goal setting: *Where do you want to be?*

3. Plan creation: *How will you get there?*

4. Execution: *Take action and make it happen.*

5. Reassessment: *Repeat the process regularly.*

Use the worksheet in Appendix C to complete your personal financial plan.

WHAT IF I'M NOT REALLY A FINANCE TYPE OF PERSON?

No matter what your profession or path in life, you have to manage your personal finances. This isn't about what you like or don't like to do. This is what you must do to take control of your life and your destiny. If you've fooled yourself into thinking that because you're "creative," or "an artist," or a "social entrepreneur" you don't have to worry about money, then just quit now. No, seriously. Stop reading, because you clearly missed the part about reflecting upon and identifying the lies you might be telling yourself.

If you're "not really a finance type of person," then make yourself one, and quickly! That type of mentality is not how a wealthy, successful man thinks. If you've convinced yourself God will provide, you'll just hit the lottery one day, blah, blah, blah, then this book—*all the books in the world*—won't help you.

AFFIRM

I have an appetite for continuous learning.

You might be uncomfortable hearing that, but as your sister in personal finance success I just had to tell you. It is what it is. And if you're not ready, all I ask is that you not toss me up on the shelf. At least pass me on to someone you know that's ready to be a finance type of person.

WHAT IS THE MOST IMPORTANT FINANCIAL PRINCIPLE I SHOULD KNOW?

I probably sound like a broken record, but the most important financial principle to remember is that to achieve success in your finances, your mindset toward wealth creation must be on the correct setting. Your thoughts about, actions with, and feelings about money must be shaped on the inside before positive results manifest on the outside.

Your roots create your fruits. No matter how much money you accumulate in your life, if you're not ready to receive it on the inside, your outside will never allow you to keep it. Being financially sound means having being determined to seek out those opportunities to learn more about what you know you don't know, as well as those things you have no idea you don't know.

Some time ago, I heard a wonderful New Year's sermon in which the pastor told us we must realize how important *who you are* is in relationship to setting goals for where you want to go and what you want to have. The pastor explained that many people have gifts and talents that will take them to celebrated places in life—places where their characters can never maintain nor sustain them.

Is that deep or what? Think about the entertainers, athletes, and other lauded figures who've amassed great fortunes only to end up on *E! True Hollywood Story* explaining how they lost it all. Don't shake your head or point your finger. You're no different! If you don't dig deep and strengthen your roots now, tomorrow's fruits will be the same old fruits you've always gotten, and while the life you desire may be attainable, it will never be sustainable.

If you plan to be successful on this journey, which will often require sacrifices, then you must make up your mind right now that where you want to go and who you want to be outweigh what anyone else thinks about you. Decide now that you will maintain a "whatever it takes" attitude. Resolve that you won't waste time worrying about what anyone else thinks of your plan.

UN REAL
More than 70% of Americans are living paycheck to paycheck.

Understand that on this journey you must refuse to be "normal," living paycheck to paycheck like most Americans. Decide today that you will take control of your mindset in order to take control of your life. *Are you ready?*

HOW DO YOU DEFINE WEALTH?

The dictionary defines wealth this way:

> **wealth** (wlth) *n.*
> 1. **a.** An abundance of valuable material possessions or
>   resources; riches.
>   **b.** The state of being rich; affluence.
> 2. All goods and resources having value in terms of exchange or use.
> 3. A great amount; a profusion: *a wealth of advice.*

I've also heard many different explanations of wealth from a biblical standpoint. Some are positive, but many offer a negative view, portraying rich people as miserable and painting a picture of the unspeakable joy of the poor.

When deciding what you choose to believe, consider the following questions.

- *If God gave us the ability to produce wealth, why would it be evil?*
- *God calls upon you to help the poor, but how can you help them if you can't meet your own needs?*
- *God calls you to leave an inheritance to your children's children, but how can you possibly do that if you have more debt than you do assets?*

I choose to believe God wants me to be wealthy because of the value I add to His people, and I will be a good steward of all that I'm blessed to receive.

You can create your own definition of wealth. After all, it sets the foundation for how *you* move forward, so get clear about it, and quickly!

HOW DO I SET FINANCIAL GOALS I CAN ACHIEVE?

There's a distinct difference between hoping, wishing, dreaming, and even praying for the things you want and actually setting goals that help you achieve your financial dreams.

When most people set financial goals, they sound something like this:

- *I want to improve my credit score.*
- *I'd like to save more.*
- *It would be nice to pay off debt.*

Those dry, bland, and grossly vague goals don't work when you're looking for long-term success. Pretending they can actually effect change in your life is a waste of time. I've been accused in the past of being a little harsh on this subject—okay, sometimes a lot harsh—but the question you must ask yourself is "Do I want to rattle off random and generic goals just to hear myself talk, or do I want to set goals I can actually achieve and use to change my life?" If you choose the latter, then keep reading.

Real TALK

Undefined goals are nothing more than dream killers.

1. **BE SPECIFIC.** So you want to improve your credit, save money, and pay off bills? Great! Join the club. What do you really want to achieve though? Undefined goals are dream killers. In order to achieve your financial goals you must be deliberate about your intentions and use concrete numbers to gauge your success. Write down the goal, and be clear about dollar amounts, percentages, and dates for accomplishment.

   For example:
   GOAL 1: I will improve my median credit score by forty points by June 1st of this year.
   GOAL 2: I will add $1200 to my opportunity fund by December 31st of this year.
   GOAL 3: I will pay off $2120 of debt and eliminate one credit card and three medical bills by December 31st of this year.

2. **BE DELIBERATE.** So you have great quantitative goals now, but how will you reach them? It's always easier to divide a large task into smaller steps, so you're not overwhelmed. To achieve your goals, get in the habit of creating "next steps" on a quarterly, monthly, or even weekly basis, depending upon your goal. As you cross off action items on your smaller list, continue to add additional steps until your goal is reached. Every Monday, I determine what wins I want to create in the week by listing "What's Important Now" on my to-do list. This allows me to track my

progress and make sure I don't overlook anything I need to do to reach my current goals.

For example:

GOAL 1 ACTION: Request a copy of my annual credit report by January 10th.

GOAL 2 ACTION: Identify three budget areas where I can save a combined $100 per month by February 15th.

GOAL 3 ACTION: Call creditors and negotiate more favorable interest rates or repayment terms by February 1st.

3. **BE ACCOUNTABLE.** You've got your big goals all worked out, and you even have action steps to keep you moving along, but if you don't achieve your goals, who will know? Well, that's where accountability comes in to play. Accountability is probably the single greatest motivator for achieving your dreams. Most people won't share their dreams with anyone for fear of failing in front of friends and family. If no one knows you had a goal, then no one will know you failed, right?

   That's the worst attitude to have. It may sound cliché, but to be successful, you need the support and encouragement of someone in your life. Whether it's a dear friend or close family member, share your dreams with someone you trust, and let them help you help yourself.

WHY SHOULD I CARE ABOUT WHAT'S GOING ON IN THE ECONOMY?

You can't live like your household economy is independent of the nation's economic trials and triumphs. Stay aware of what goes on in the real world because it has a huge impact on your personal life. This isn't to say that if the national economy is in a slump, you have to be, but it may affect job opportunities you're banking on, timing for the launch your new business idea, or how your investments perform.

Being financially sound will give you the ability to weather the ups and downs of the national economy. Planning, saving, and investing wisely will help you weather economic hard times. Unlike a staggering number of Americans, you'll be ready to withstand the storm because you already live beneath your means, debt-free, and with plenty of money in savings to support yourself should you encounter job loss or any other financially devastating occurrence.

My husband, Gerald, and I learned all this the hard way. We started our first business at twenty-two and twenty-one years old, when the real estate market was booming. Experts had long forewarned that the housing bubble was likely to burst, but the money kept rolling in, and being young and naïve, we refused to heed economists' predictions. When it was all said and done, the bubble did burst, and a lot of us in the industry were left soaking wet! I wish we would've gotten out earlier, but at least we had eighteen months of savings for that very rainy season.

WHAT OTHER RESOURCES SHOULD I USE TO GET CONTROL OF MY FINANCES (AND INCOME)?

Read material from a diverse group of personal finance experts. Most will have a different way of delivering a similar message. The goal is just that you take action and do something! I've been reading about this stuff for years, and there's not a single interpretation I agree with 100%. Take what works for you, and feel free to leave behind the parts that don't.

You'll find a complete list of resources I recommend in Appendix A.

EARN MORE MONEY

"Talent is never enough. With few exceptions the best players are the hardest workers." - Earvin "Magic" Johnson

THE RECIPE FOR FINANCIAL success is simple: the highest income you can achieve coupled with the lowest expenses you can maintain for your personal standard or preferred quality of life. When I speak about earning more money, most people assume I'm encouraging entrepreneurship. As an aspiring entrepreneur since the second grade and a working entrepreneur since my husband and I founded and managed a real estate, mortgage, investment, and escrow brokerage when I was just twenty-one years old, it's no secret I believe in using your gifts and strengths to create income by owning a business.

I do push entrepreneurship quite a bit. Study the professional athletes who managed their money wisely and used it to transition into entrepreneurship. They continue to earn substantial income, sometimes more than they did as players, after their pro careers end. Their peers who don't take similar action often struggle financially.

Entrepreneurship is great for many people, but it's not the only way to prosper. You can grow where you're planted and make the very most of a more conventional career path. When professional athletes hold out for higher salaries during contract negotiations, a lot of people gripe and call them greedy. Naysayers complain that we pay quarterbacks, like Brett

Favre who became the NFL's first $100 million player, obscene amounts of money, while schoolteachers and police officers are underpaid. What the critics forget is that every person has the right to make as much money as he possibly can in his job, regardless of what he does for a living. A smart athlete demonstrates his value to the team and then does what he can to maximize his income. When you work for someone else, you should take steps to contribute as much as possible, be recognized for your contribution, and be compensated with the highest possible salary.

Whether you're running your own business or working in someone else's, the lessons in this section will help you earn more money by fulfilling your purpose. Deuteronomy 8:18 reminds us God is the one who gives us the gifts we can use to produce wealth. He's given you all you need to earn more money. It's up to you to identify those gifts and use them strategically.

AFFIRM

I admire wealthy and successful people.

WORKPLACE WISDOM

A LOT OF PEOPLE COME from environments where the main purpose of work is survival, and not necessarily to thrive or grow professionally. Depending on your upbringing, you may or may not struggle from time to time with navigating the unspoken rules of the business world, but there's a lot you can do to make the most of your job and improve your position. It simply requires learning and implementing a little workplace wisdom.

HOW CAN I TRANSITION TO A JOB I LOVE
WHEN I'M RESPONSIBLE FOR A FAMILY?

It may feel noble to sacrifice your dreams to work in a job you don't like so you can take care of your family. But would you want your kids trudging off every day to a job they hate? You don't have to give up your idea of a dream job for the greater good of your family. With sound planning, you can make the transition without placing your family at risk. And you'll give your children an example of what it looks like to go to work loving what you do and earning a sufficient income at the same time.

Research what it would take to transition to the job you love. If it pays a lower salary, then you may need to put more money in savings and figure out where your family can downsize and cut back on expenses. Even better, figure out how to maximize your income in that new position. In the meantime, consider working part-time in the industry you want to switch to, so you can see if it really is a good fit.

WHY HAVEN'T I FOUND MY DREAM JOB?

It's extremely hard to find something when you're not exactly sure what you're looking for. Maybe you're used to rattling off a list of things you hate or would like to change about your current employment, but have you taken time to sit down and imagine what your dream job would entail? It could be right under your nose in your current company. Or your dream may not even exist in your industry, which means you need to start looking elsewhere. Listen. Even if you earn more money doing what you do now, if you aren't happy or fulfilled, you'll just find a way to mismanage what you earn.

You have a right to do work that you love. In our society, we seem to think that's a privilege reserved for a select few: athletes, entertainers, and über-wealthy business people. Aren't you tired of hearing how *they're* living the life of their dreams, when you can't say the same thing yet? Don't you deserve to have the same kind of happiness and fulfillment?

Whether you work on your own or for someone else, it's imperative that you engage in work you love. When you get clarity around what you actually want in your dream job, you create the space to receive what you desire. That's not to say what you want will magically appear, but you can become intentional with your speech and strategic with the activities you engage in and the people with whom you choose to associate.

Take a moment to find clarity by answering these questions. Remember to write your answers down in a journal of some sort. Capturing your responses, rather than just thinking about them, will help you do a deeper analysis and create a record to refer back to in the future.

- *What do I really want to do? (What do I do best with the least amount of effort? What brings me joy? What would I do for a living, if money were not a factor?)*
- *Who do I really want to work with as clients and/or co-workers?*
- *What types of activities will I be responsible for on a day-to-day basis?*
- *Where will I work? (home office, executive office, Starbucks)*

- *What will my work schedule look like? (days off, hours per day, etc.)*

DRAFT A DESCRIPTION OF YOUR DREAM JOB.

If what you described is at all possible in your current work environment, complete this section. If you're convinced that the job you want is completely impossible to find in your current work environment, skip to: *How do I know when it's time to find new employment?*

WHAT CAN I DO TO GET NOTICED FOR THE JOB I WANT?

Figuring out how to climb the ladder within your company is no easy task. You bust your butt doing good work, but you still get passed over for the promotions for which you're clearly qualified. Well, let's talk about what you can start doing immediately to get noticed and prevent another opportunity from passing you by!

1. **GET CLEAR ABOUT YOUR TRUE VALUE.** This is not about what you "feel" like you contribute to the team. Identify your contributions and be able to quantify them at a moment's notice. Measure your successes in terms of cost savings, increased productivity, and overall contribution to the company. Did you save your department $34,000 this quarter? Are you already at 96% of your annual goal? No team wants to lose their most valuable player, and similarly no company wants to lose their most talented employee. Be crystal clear, first with yourself and then with the powers that be, about what qualities you bring to the table.

    Real MONEY

    Quantify your professional value to make a case for promotion or salary increase.

2. **LET YOUR BOSS KNOW YOU WANT TO MOVE UP.** Learn how to effectively articulate your goals. Don't assume your manager or supervisor knows you're interested in another position. Your boss might believe you're 100% comfortable doing what you've been doing all this time, especially when you're so darn good at it! Ask for a face-to-face meeting rather than attempting to present your case in a letter or via e-mail. One-way

communication doesn't allow you to develop a mutual understanding of the situation and come up with a plan of action. Ask about potential opportunities for advancement, and find out how you can prepare to take advantage of them. Try to enroll your boss in your vision and use the meeting to toot your own horn a little by sharing a detailed list of your professional accomplishments.

3. **LOOK THE PART.** A mentor shared with me years ago that you dress for the job you want, *not* for the job you have. This doesn't mean you should spend extra money on clothes you can't afford, but it does mean you should do the best you can with what you have. Try not wearing jeans and sneakers just because your office is laid-back. Do you want to blend in with your co-workers or wear slacks and a sport coat, and stand a little above the rest?

Real **TALK**

Dress for the job you want, not the job you have.

4. **NETWORK ON THE JOB.** Moving ahead isn't only about who you know. It's also about who knows you! Don't reserve all of your networking skills for those awkward business networking mixers. Get to know different folks in and outside of your department. Make a friend in the HR department. Aren't they usually the first to learn of internal job postings? If another department piques your interest, seek out information about what's going on and how things work there. Let the department's manager know you're interested in learning more and would even be willing to come in after hours or on an off day to help out. As long as it doesn't affect your performance in your current position, your manager shouldn't be upset, and you'll let everyone know you're definitely the one to watch for the next big opening.

Most people sit around complaining and waiting to be noticed. Be willing to go beyond what the average person is willing to do, and expect the best. Get clear, get vocal, get connected, and get noticed for the job you want!

HOW DO I NEGOTIATE A HIGHER SALARY?

Earning more money may not mean an entrepreneurial effort for you. It might be as simple and strategic as negotiating a raise on your current job. Before you can do that though, let's be clear. The typical employee only works hard enough so they don't get fired, and their boss pays them just enough so they don't quit. If you're on your second warning for coming into the office late, submitting incomplete work, or anything you know in your soul is workplace suicide, and you're still there merely by God's grace, this information won't help you. But if you've been on your game, ask yourself these questions to prepare for your next salary negotiation.

Real TALK

If you only work hard enough to avoid getting fired, you're in no position to ask for a raise.

1. **WHY NOW?** To draft a good game plan, you have to understand the *why* behind what you're doing, or your efforts will be scattered and ineffective. Ask yourself plenty of questions to get to the root of why you want, need, and deserve a raise or promotion. The fact that you're behind on bills could be a motivation for you, but it won't be enough to sway your superiors. Is there a position coming available for which you truly qualify? Are you hoping you can have a position created based on extra duties you're already performing?

2. **WHY AM I VALUABLE?** You've been patted on the back and told you were great in the past, but have you really kept a running list of your own accomplishments? If not, it's time to start a "brag folder." Keep all positive reviews, notes of appreciation, thank you cards, and anything that can support your effort all together in a place you can access immediately. Your goal is to become crystal clear about what qualities you bring to the table, so you can learn to articulate them effectively. You don't want to appear entitled or cocky, but you should toot your own horn when and where it's appropriate.

    Quantify your successes in terms of cost savings, increased productivity, and overall contribution to the company. Never just say you hit your annual goals back in September. Make sure everyone knows that to date, you're at 125% of your goal and counting. Now that's value, especially when others are struggling to hit 70%! It's also a lot more professional than saying, "I do more work than so-and-so."

3. **WHERE'S MY RESEARCH?** You have to know as much as you can about the pay scale of the company, as well as that of the industry. Check out sites like www.salary.com or www.payscale.com, which collect salary and career data from millions of people across thousands of industries to give you accurate salary averages narrowed down to your metropolitan area. If you're maxed out for your job, then the reality is that it may be time to go after another position. If you haven't hit the ceiling, then you're stockpiling serious ammunition!

4. **WHO SHOULD I TALK TO?** In some work environments, where there's only one manager or you report directly to the owner of the business, this is pretty obvious. Other companies are layered with an overwhelming chain of command. While you might think it makes sense to go straight to your supervisor, remember that although they may adore you, they likely don't control the budget.

   It may make sense to speak with your human resources department first to assess what your options are. Often, they can give you helpful tips on how salary increases or promotions are typically given. Now remember, this is not an opportunity to go and complain about how overworked and underpaid you are. As much as HR is supposed to maintain confidentiality, the reality is that people talk. Don't let something negative get back to your manager before you have a chance to present your thorough and well-researched case.

5. **WHAT SHOULD I OFFER?** Oh, you thought you could ask for something without offering to give something? Not quite. Giving you additional income might mean the bottom line for the business will receive less income. If you've been denied an increase in the past, maybe the numbers just didn't make sense. If you're ready to explain how to make this a win-win situation, you may actually have a shot. The most positive way to approach a request for a raise is to ask for extra work and responsibility. You can link this to a pay increase, if not immediately, then in the future. Employers

AFFIRM

I boldly walk through life displaying confidence.

respond to this approach better than simply asking for more pay for doing the exact same job. Additionally, you might want to ask for a performance-related bonus or increase, subject to generating more output than current or expected levels.

6. **HOW AND WHEN SHOULD I ASK?** Ask for a face-to-face meeting rather than attempting to present your case in a letter or via e-mail. Either of these is just a one-way communication and won't allow you to develop a mutual understanding of the situation and what to do about it. It can also be perceived as a demand, no matter how politely you try word it. After all, written content is always left up to the perception of the reader, not necessarily the intent of the writer.

If you have a review coming up, you can wait until then, but if not, simply ask your boss for a review meeting. Never say, "I want to talk to you about a raise." No one will be clearing their calendar for that conversation. In the meeting, ask what opportunities for advancement are coming up and how you can to prepare to take advantage of them. Ask what flexibilities exist and what the standard is for setting and increasing pay levels. Who does your boss have to make a case to? Will he or she support you? What would improve your case? What commitments would the company want from you? What can you put in, and what can be given in return? Approach the process positively and constructively, and remember it's a discussion, not a demand.

If you're unhappy with your salary, and you feel underpaid or undervalued, you'll do your reputation and future a lot of good by approaching the matter in a professional, well-prepared, and objective way.

WHAT DOES MY PERSONAL LIFE HAVE TO DO WITH MY PROFESSIONAL LIFE?

When you hear Apple, BMW, Coca-Cola, or Wal-Mart, you automatically create specific images in your head about each one of those brands and what they represent. Likewise, very specific images come up when you hear names like Beyoncé, Cher, or Michael Jackson.

Brands aren't just for businesses; they're also for people. It's important to understand that you always represent your brand. There's absolutely no way to separate your personal and professional brands. Just think of the late Whitney Houston or athlete Michael Vick. What they may have considered "personal business" still managed to damage their professional brands. While some can bounce back, many never do.

Let's tackle three areas where your personal life impacts your professional brand.

1. **YOUR APPEARANCE AND ATTIRE.** What does your appearance say about you? Remember that dressing appropriately isn't reserved for the days you go into the office. Any place you go has the potential to produce an ideal client, business partnership, or new contract. Do you start each day expecting opportunities to come your way? If so, there's no such thing as just "running out." You never know who you might run into. You may not always be aware of it, but there's always someone watching who has the potential to bless you.

    It never fails. I run into former students at Target, furniture stores, Starbucks, and even the airport! I doubt a single one of them can say I've had to apologize or make an excuse for my appearance.

2. **YOUR SOCIAL MEDIA PROFILES.** What do your tweets, pictures, and status updates say about you? If you're an attorney, but every picture of you on social media portrays you as a drunken party animal, how seriously do you expect potential clients to take you? People who are considering doing business with you will search far beyond your LinkedIn profile. Yes, we see your crisp white shirt and new suit on LinkedIn, and yes, you've managed to scrape together a pretty impressive paragraph or two about your experience, but consumers are smarter these days. We know the truth about you exists in your late night tweets and your Facebook albums, and even if you restrict them to family and friends, pictures and posts can be downloaded and shared.

Pay attention to what your friends post to your page too. If there's profanity, links to the latest big-booty-girls website, or anything that could be considered inappropriate on your page or in the comments, people will judge you by it.

3.   **YOUR ASSOCIATES AND EXTRACURRICULAR ACTIVITIES.** What do your friends say about you? Again, your network determines your net worth. Period. When you're out and about, who do people see you hanging out with? Whatever perception others have of your associates, they'll also have of you. Like Grandma always said, "Birds of a feather flock together." If you're investing a lot of time with folks that aren't going where you desire to go, then you're setting yourself back.

Make sure you're seen at networking events relevant to your industry. Invest your time in people and activities that support your dreams and goals and put you in front of and around people who have brands that can add credibility to the brand you're developing.

Building your personal and professional brand takes time, a little maintenance, and enough self-control to filter what you share on social media. Regardless of the sacrifice, brand development is a part of the process that prepares you for your destiny and sets you up to earn more money. Now what's more exciting than that?

DO NICE GUYS FINISH LAST AT WORK?

According to a 2011 study, men who were "less agreeable" earned about 18% more than peers who described themselves with words like "warm" and "caring." Does this mean you should go to work kicking in doors and acting like a jerk? Probably not. Rather than a raving psychopath causing all types of workplace disruptions, a disagreeable person is "more likely . . . to behave disagreeably in certain situations by, for instance, aggressively advocating for their position during conflicts." With that being

People who are "ruder" in the workplace earn about 5% more than their peers.

People do business with people they like. Learn to build relationships to get ahead.

said, you have to wonder if what they're really describing is reasonable assertiveness.

Either way, here are a few tips to keep in mind as you strive to earn that extra 18% and more.

1. **PROVIDE OUTSTANDING WORK.** Always present work you can be proud of and stand behind 100%. Most people will still value work ethic, whether they see you as warm and kind or not.

2. **BE LIKEABLE.** People do business with folks they like, so let's not go overboard on the assertiveness. One of the best lessons I learned from my mother is that you really do catch more flies with honey. As a businessman, one of your best traits may be your assertiveness, but you also have to manage relationships well. You can get what you need from people without demeaning, bullying, and being totally obnoxious.

3. **VOICE YOUR OPINION CONSTRUCTIVELY.** Be passionate, not emotional. When you believe the team should go in a certain direction, research the facts and state your case in a well-thought-out manner. If the team decides to go in another direction, accept it and know that you gave it your all. And if it turns out you were right, everyone will remember that and hopefully seek out your wisdom in the future.

4. **STAND UP FOR YOURSELF.** Sometimes you have to take a stand instead of trying to keep the peace. You may be able to display leadership skills no one knew you had, which can pay off professionally and monetarily.

5. **KEEP INVESTING IN YOUR PERSONAL AND PROFESSIONAL DEVELOPMENT.** It's almost impossible to not earn more as you learn more and, most importantly, put what you learn into practice. There's just a certain confidence that comes with knowing that you know what you know! That doesn't mean you don't remain teachable or coachable, but the point of learning is to use what you know to positively impact both your personal performance and the bottom line of your organization.

6. **CREATE YOUR OWN PERSONAL STANDARD FOR SUCCESS.** When you set your own goals, you're not as worried about acting on every new study published

or what labels you should apply to your personality. Know who you are, and be consistently confident in what you bring to the table.

HOW DO I DEAL WITH COMPETITION IN THE WORKPLACE?

Many men are competitive by nature, and that competitive spirit can come out in the workplace in the form of someone trying to move in on your position, your territory, or your connections. Instead of doing the hard work to earn his own place, he wants to slide in and take over what you've built.

The key to maintaining what you've earned is consistent excellence. Be so good, people have to recognize your work and give you credit, even if they do so grudgingly. Regardless of how other people behave, continue to perform with integrity. At the same time, I like the advice of my personal business coach, Lisa Nichols, a best-selling author, international speaker, and CEO, who says, "I take nothing personally, but I take note of everything."

HOW DO I KNOW WHEN IT'S TIME TO FIND NEW EMPLOYMENT?

You really don't need me or anyone else to tell you when it's time to move on from a job. You've known it in your gut for some time now. And guess what? According to several studies, you're not alone. Only 19% of American workers say they're actually satisfied with their jobs. The majority are serious when they say they're working strictly to get a paycheck, and you may feel the same way.

UN REAL

Less than 25% of American workers say they're satisfied with their jobs.

Let's see how the following questions resonate with you.

- *Were you passed over for yet another promotion only to watch someone with less seniority, talent, and commitment slide into the position?*
- *Do you wake up excited to make a difference on your job or dreading the fact that it's yet another work day?*

- *Do you start the week celebrating Monday or looking forward to Friday?*
- *Do you find yourself daydreaming in meetings and having to ask people what you missed?*
- *Do you get physically ill or mentally exhausted from the mere mention of your job or anyone associated with it?*

Did any of those ring a bell, even a little? I see men working at jobs that make them miserable or keep them under constant pressure all too often. And all too often, I see the deadly consequences of that choice. Recently, a friend of our family, a young man in his mid-thirties, suffered a fatal heart attack. He had an office job with long hours. He was underpaid and often had to work weeks at a time without a day off to relax and spend time with his family. Even as people warned him that no job was worth dying for, he felt he had to stay in the position to support his family. Now his three precious children will grow up without a father. Talk about a wake-up call for anyone making that same choice every day.

If you've ever thought to yourself, "I hate this job, but I'm doing this for my family," think about how your family will get along if they lose you. That young man's story is just one of many I've heard, but your story doesn't need to have the same ending. Trust me. Your kids would rather give up some of their luxuries while you transition out of a bad job than see that empty seat at football games and dance recitals.

Am I saying you should run out and quit your job tomorrow? Of course not. Take baby steps and plan properly, but don't wait. You need to do whatever it takes to find or create the job environment that will keep you fulfilled.

(See: *Why haven't I found my dream job?*)

LAUNCH YOUR BUSINESS WHILE YOU WORK

MANY MEN COME TO me feeling frustrated, overworked, underpaid, and unfulfilled. Over and over again, I hear from prospective clients who say they're tired of working hard to build someone else's business, while their salaries remain pretty much the same no matter how much effort they put in. Sound familiar?

For some people, entrepreneurship is a lifelong dream, but for others the desire to launch a business stems from getting fed up with all things workplace associated. Either way, when your personal finances are in disarray, it's very hard to take that leap of faith, a common situation that often leaves people stuck in dead-end jobs. To make matters worse, many men feel like they can't risk entrepreneurship when so many people depend on them financially.

The best way to mitigate the risk of going out on your own is to launch your business while you still have your job. NBA superstar Earvin "Magic" Johnson knew early in life that he wanted to be an entrepreneur. Unlike many professional athletes, he didn't wait until after he retired from basketball to launch his first business venture. Instead, he started while he had the security of a regular paycheck and built his first enterprise while he worked his full-time job. And no, you don't have to be earning NBA money to start your business while you work. People of average income are doing it every day. Gerald M., a dedicated member of our armed forces stationed overseas and one of the men in the focus group which helped to create this book, shared that he gets involved in business now not by working on any day to day operations because he can't. He does, however, invest in and make money from business ventures by providing capital, helping to steer the vision and goals of the companies he creates with his partners and just being keen to negotiating and seizing opportunities in general. He calls it a win-win. While Gerald M. is doing the day to day work for his job, he's also being paid to get his own personal affairs, goals, aspirations and short and long-term goals in order now instead of waiting for retirement.

HOW COULD I POSSIBLY START A BUSINESS AND KEEP WORKING?

Every day I coach clients who are waiting until their schedules clear up, waiting to get their children through college, waiting to save a little more money, or waiting for some person, place, or thing outside of themselves to bring their entrepreneurial dreams to fruition. When I ask why not go after their dreams *now*, the number one answer is that they work full-time.

Real MONEY

Starting a business while you work your job allows you to test the waters while you're still getting a paycheck.

It's the glass half full or half empty scenario. Maybe your job is in the way, but it could be the blessing you need to test out the viability of a new business while you have the consistency of a steady job. My father-in-law always said, "Nobody likes to do business with desperate people." The security of a steady paycheck can keep you from becoming that desperate person constantly reducing his price or giving an annoyingly needy sales pitch to try to get business. In the book, *Hustle While You Work*, the author, Hotep, explains "Your job is not an obstacle in the way of your entrepreneurial dream; your job is the way to your entrepreneurial dream."

If we'd all been taught how to hustle *while* we work, I truly believe many of us would've stayed afloat longer when the economy suffered the major setbacks of the Great Recession. Far more people could have sustained mortgages, car notes, and college tuition for much longer if they hadn't been dependent on a single income stream.

If we were taught more about creating passive income (income that does not come from active participation in a business) instead of believing we could still simply "go to college and get a job," we'd be much further along as a country.

In addition to already having a full-time job, there are several other common excuses many people use to avoid starting a side hustle while they work. Make sure you're not letting these excuses hold you back.

1. **I DON'T HAVE TIME.** You make time for the things you want to make time for. You don't *find* time, as if it were hiding around a corner or under a mattress somewhere. Turn off the game, get off Facebook and YouTube, and stop wasting time complaining about all the stuff you wish you had time to do.

    If you get focused and organize and prioritize your daily activities, you can easily begin to hustle while you work!

2. **ALL THE GOOD IDEAS ARE GONE.** I'm a firm believer that we're all born to fulfill some purpose in life. We're each blessed with unique gifts, talents, and abilities to bring to the marketplace. No one's saying your big idea has to be the next Facebook. You can create additional income and live a fulfilling life by doing something that's already been done. Whether it's already been done or not, if it's never been done by you, then there's still an opportunity. Don't quit before you start.

    Assess your gifts, talents, and skills, and figure out a way to put your own unique spin on them, so you can begin to hustle while you work.

3. **I'M JUST NOT READY.** What are you waiting for? Perfect timing? Progress beats perfection any day. No matter how many books and blogs you read, or how many informational interviews you do, there will always be more to learn. If I worried about completely understanding blog monetization before I started my blog, you wouldn't be reading this book right now.

When it comes to building a business, progress beats perfection any day.

Pool all of the information and resources you have under your belt, and just get started! When you do your part, trust me, God or the Universe or whoever you recognize as your higher source, will bring forth everything else you need. It all starts with you!

If nothing else, I hope the recent economic instability has convinced you that your path to financial independence and a secure future can only be found by tapping into your own abilities. If you have a job, be grateful because many people don't. But don't use it as an excuse not to start your own business. Use it as a stepping stone, and hustle while you work.

REFLECT | What excuses have you used to delay moving forward with your business idea? Do you recognize now why those really are just excuses?

HOW AM I SUPPOSED TO BALANCE A JOB, A SIDE-BUSINESS, AND A FAMILY?

Wake up. People all over this country do it every day. I was one of them for nearly two years, so you won't get much sympathy from me. I wrote two books while I worked full-time counseling hundreds of men and women on credit and money management at a nonprofit agency. At the same time, I also maintained my blog, wrote for magazines, did private coaching, and managed the hectic schedules of my traveling husband and a small child with more activities and appointments than the average adult.

Do many people consider that type of schedule crazy? Absolutely. But do you want the results and approval of the average person? Or do you want the results other successful people get? It all boils down to what your priorities are. When something is important to you, you make time to do it. It just so happens in my case I loved my job, because it was truly a dream job for me. I'm also extremely passionate about my business, and the well-being of my family is of the utmost importance to me. At the time, there was no room to say no or to slack off in any of these areas.

AFFIRM

I have everything I need to get where I'm going.

Contrary to popular belief, I actually did sleep, and eat, and occasionally have fun. I just did what I learned to do while maintaining a hectic schedule and going to college. I prioritized.

Understanding how to prioritize is the key to balancing everything your heart desires. As long as you're disciplined, you don't have to short-change any area of life.

Here are a few ways you can create discipline and balance in your life.

1. **KEEP A WRITTEN CALENDAR OR APPOINTMENT BOOK.** With smartphones and tablets in your hands all day, it's easy to forget the importance of writing down activities and being able to physically see your week or month at a glance.

    I'm not opposed to using apps, but writing down information helps you remember your obligations and easily see the openings where business or social activities can be added.

2. **START ASSIGNMENTS IN ADVANCE.** Stay ahead of the game on your work and you'll never have to worry about other parts of your life interfering with last-minute assignments. If you have orders to fill, or in my world, deadlines for article submissions, always stay one week ahead. Even if you have to cram in some work time, the less you have to do twenty-four to forty-eight hours before the due date, the better.

3. **ORGANIZE EVERY PART OF YOUR LIFE.** The more organized you are, the better. Here are a few things I do to organize and add structure to my life.

    •   **USE BLOCK SCHEDULING.** Only do certain work-related activities at certain times or on certain days. For example, Mondays are my writing days. I don't coach or take meetings or work on business development. All I do is write. It helps me stay focused and productive, as opposed to jumping around from project to project. You may want to decide that you only return emails or phone calls at certain times throughout the day. Putting time constraints on activities will help you regain control of your schedule.

    •   **PREPARE IN ADVANCE.** We iron and lay out my daughter's clothes for the week on Sunday nights and pack her lunches and snacks the night before each school day. This routine works as well for adults as it does for children, and it saves time and frustration for the whole family. After nearly missing—okay, actually missing—flights in the past, Gerald and I finally learned to pull together a travel wardrobe at least seventy-two hours in advance and to use packing lists for our business trips each week. These days, we simply zip up the suitcase and go. But before we implemented this system, our travel was a nightmare. These simple changes have saved us a lot of time and frustration!

UN REAL

The average person wastes 153 days of his or her lifetime looking for misplaced items.

- **PUT EVERYTHING IN THE SAME PLACE EVERY TIME.** According to a 2012 study, the average person spends a total of 3,680 hours, or 153 days, over a lifetime looking for misplaced stuff. That's nearly two years of forty-hour work weeks that could be invested directly into your new business just by keeping things in order.

- **LEARN TO SAY NO MORE OFTEN.** Pressure from friends, family, or co-workers can make you feel like you're either obligated to do things or that you're missing out on all the fun. Creating the life you want has to outweigh the opinions of others, who may not agree with or understand your vision. Sure, you'll have to sacrifice a little now to get where you want to go later. If your dreams are big enough, isn't the sacrifice worth it?

HOW DO I EVEN KNOW WHAT I'M GOOD AT?

In my *Mindset + Money Master Class*®, I teach students how to discover what they're good at by helping them understand their Sweet Spot. Now,

Real MONEY

Your Sweet Spot is the intersection between your gifts and skills and what the market will pay you for them.

before you go getting any ideas, let me explain. The Sweet Spot is simply the intersection between your gifts and skills and what the marketplace will actually pay you for possessing those qualities and packaging them properly.

The first step in recognizing your Sweet Spot is to assess gifts and talents.

Write your answers to the following questions.

- *What do you do better than anyone else around you with the least amount of effort?*
- *On what subjects are people constantly asking you for advice?*
- *What gives you energy?*
- *What are you happiest doing? With whom? When?*

HOW CAN I MAKE MONEY FROM MY HOBBY?

Every change starts in the mind. Every change starts with a decision. First, decide to stop calling your gifts and talents "hobbies" if you truly desire to make money using them. It's time for your thinking and your speech to shift. You're no longer the person who fixes everything for free or the one who can do this or that for "whatever you want to give me."

Visit sites like sba.gov or score.org to find free business plan templates.

Dee-jaying, photography, videography, wood working, fitness, coaching Little League—almost anything you've treated as a hobby has the potential to become a business. From the most specialized service to the simplest task, there's someone out there who needs what you have to offer. They just have to know you're ready, willing, and able to do it. No matter how small or large your business idea, write out a business plan because If you fail to plan, you're planning to fail. You can find business plan templates on sites like www.sba.gov or www.score.org, but don't be overwhelmed by the process. The point is to get a basic plan on paper keep moving forward, not get caught up in the planning stage.

Answer the questions below, along with the gift assessment in the previous section (*How do I even know what I'm good at?*), and get to the fundamentals of how to profit from your hobby. Momentum is a beautiful thing. Just start.

IDENTIFY YOUR SKILL SET.
Answer the following questions in your journal.

- *What degrees or certifications have you earned?* They don't have to be directly connected to your passion or hobby.

- *What work experience do you have? Where have you volunteered and in what role?*
- *How can you use your other experiences and skills to market your products or services?* This is your opportunity to think outside the box and use your personality and experiences to make your business stand out from the crowd. A former college baseball player could say his product or service will "hit a homerun for you every time". The point is to choose something unique about you and use it to make your business stand out.

UNDERSTAND THE MARKETPLACE AND YOUR MARKETING.

You can have the best idea in the world, but if no one knows you or your idea exists, you'll never get off the ground. And when your target audience doesn't know you're speaking directly to them, you're finished before you start.

Who specifically makes up the market for your product or service? Just saying it's for men isn't enough. A man of what age, income, religion, and marital status? Does he have children? A college degree? What kind of car does he drive? What music does he listen to? Go deep, and get specific.

Where are these men? What types of places do they frequent? How do they typically receive information? List at least seven low-cost methods you can use to get your message to your ideal customer, such as a blog, Facebook, Twitter, an e-zine, or a newsletter.

WHAT IF I DON'T HAVE SALES EXPERIENCE?

The great part about connecting with your purpose and creating a business with your natural gift is that you're never selling anything. Look at it as simply sharing your gift with the world. When you believe you're doing what you were born to do, you radiate passion. Your ears perk up at the mere mention of anything related to your field, and your eyes light up with a spark of infectious enthusiasm. You begin to naturally talk a about it or get drawn into conversations on the topic.

$ Real MONEY

When you're passionate about sharing your gifts through your business, you never have to worry about selling.

Your primary job, beyond perfecting your skills, is to train yourself to talk about them in a clear and concise way that says, "I'm ready and open for business." What you've probably done in the past, like many of us, is brush off your skill or expertise as no big deal and allow others to pick up on your passion and enthusiasm, only to abuse it by paying you little to nothing.

To take the focus off selling yourself and closing the deal, try the following strategies.

1. **FOCUS ON RELATIONSHIPS.** When you focus on getting to know potential clients, they have the opportunity to decide for themselves that they want to work with you. You've likely heard, "People do business with people they know, like, and trust." Depending on your product or service, you may need to factor a "getting to know you" period into your engagement of potential customers. While building trust, you're also finding ways to stay in front of them and ensure that when they are in the market for your product or services, they immediately think of you.

2. **BECOME THE EXPERT.** Really work to become known for one specific product, service, or niche. When you do too many other things, people get confused and become unclear about how much you really know about what you're sharing. And when people don't trust your expertise, they instantly see you as someone trying to sell something.

3. **PORTRAY YOUR BRAND IN A CONSISTENT AND PROFESSIONAL MANNER.** Should your ideal client be in the market for what you have to offer, they'll come to you believing it's their privilege and honor to work with you, as opposed to you having to prove yourself to new people over and over again.

4. **THINK LIKE A MARKETER.** When you swap hats and think like a marketer, you can identify pockets of potential for your business. Once you know where your ideal customer is—what he eats, what he drives, what he wears, and many other details about him—find opportunities to get in front of him and share your gift. If you do it correctly, people will naturally be attracted to you.

WHAT CAN I DO TO MARKET MY BUSINESS?

You may feel like you don't have the time, money, or energy to market your new business venture, and that's understandable. However, you must make

If you don't have time to market your business, you need to make the time.

time for marketing. Speaking from experience, I can say with certainty that marketing my business and brand this time around has been significantly simpler and less expensive than it was ten years ago when I built my real estate firm.

Here are a few steps that will serve you well in building your brand.

1. **NETWORK RELENTLESSLY.** While you build your business, remember that your success is in the numbers. Success is not 100% about who you

Success isn't just a result of who you know; even more, it's a result of who knows you.

know. It's more about who knows you. The more people who know you exist, the better. When you network at free and low-cost events, it's not just to sell someone on your product or service. Build relationships with any and everyone, from potential clients and joint venture partners to those with complementary services and sponsors or investors. (See: *How do I network effectively?*)

2. **BUILD SOCIAL MEDIA PRESENCE.** Whether you like it or not, social media is a must-have for every new or growing business, especially since it's absolutely free. Consistent engagement is the key to using social media to benefit your business. Brainstorming a Twitter handle and creating a Facebook fan page won't be enough. Use that virtual space to speak to your target customers and prove to them by providing useful content that you know what you're talking about.

3. **BLOG ABOUT YOUR SUBJECT MATTER.** Along with building your social media presence, you need a place to send new fans for more information about you. A blog is a great free way to showcase your knowledge and build trust with your ideal clientele. Whether you write short posts, like I did when I began blogging in 2009, or highlight pictures of your work, use the blog to play up your strengths.

Like social media, your blog needs to stay fresh and updated. Don't be intimidated by bloggers who write several posts a day. Those guys are likely being paid by a sponsor to generate so much material. You may want to grow to that level at some point, but it's not necessary when you're a newbie working to discover your voice and your niche. Don't be afraid to share relevant content from other parts of the web. If you don't have any new ideas at the moment, use someone else's. Just be sure to give them credit and post a link back to their site. Your followers will appreciate that you're scouting out great information for them.

4. **FIND JOINT VENTURE PARTNERS.** In point number one of this section, I suggest networking to find joint venture partners. What you're looking for is someone who offers a product or service which complements your own. Whether live or via the internet, you two could hold events which highlight both businesses and expose each of you to the other's audience. Never fear that involving another business or brand will take business away from you. That type of thinking will prevent your business from blossoming. Remember the Universe is full of limitless abundance. This is an opportunity for you to reach people who otherwise may never know your name.

WHAT ARE THE BASIC BUSINESS LESSONS I SHOULD KNOW?

Entrepreneurship on any level is a journey, one that teaches you through trial and error. Below I've highlighted a few key concepts everyone who plans to succeed in business should know.

1. **FOCUS ON ONE THING.** As I've said, we're all blessed with unique gifts, talents, and abilities. You may be blessed with ten, but you can't focus on all ten at the same time and either expect success or expect us to buy you as the master of all things. Narrow your focus and master one thing at a time. Ultimately,

Real TALK

If you claim to be the expert on everything from relationships to real estate, no one will take you seriously.

that one thing will become a feeder for future opportunities.

Let's be real. No one trusts the man whose business card identifies him as a branding coach who sells real estate and designs custom shoes. Even if you can do all of those things, choose what you want to be known for and roll with it. Let your other hidden talents come out once a relationship is built, rather than squeezing them all on your business card.

2. **BUILD STRONG RELATIONSHIPS.** Success in business is based on the relationships you build with clientele, staff, partners, referrals, and anyone you come into contact with. No matter where I am, I greet everyone with a smile. I'm nice to people. If they have a name tag on, I honor them by saying their names and holding even a ten-second conversation, which is more than the average person takes time to give.

Someone told me once that there's always someone nearby who has the power to bless you. But will they want to if you're walking around

Real TALK

Someone with the power to bless you is always watching what you do.

with furrowed brows and a frown? Will they want to help you when you can't even say good morning to the receptionist or janitor and obviously only speak to people who you know or who you believe can do something for you? I can't tell you how many times I'm asked to speak somewhere and walk in to find people are rude or ignore me completely. Once I'm introduced as the speaker of the evening, as a person of influence, or as someone connected to others of influence, they all of a sudden want to become best friends. Of course, the opportunity for that connection has passed and will likely not come back, even if the tone has changed within a matter of minutes. First impressions are still lasting ones.

3. **LEARN THE GIFT OF GOOD-BYE.** People will come and go on your journey to success, and that's as it should be. Media mogul Tyler Perry calls them boosters. These people are there to help get your rocket off the ground. Once you've launched, it may be time for a few folks to fall off. Everyone can't handle where God is taking you, and that's okay. Accept that some people come into your life for a reason and a season. When their time is up, be content with letting them go. If they're leaving to pursue their own thing, let them go and wish them the best of luck. If you have to

kick them to the curb for being underhanded, let them go and wish them the best of luck. Whatever the reason behind their departure, understand the gift of good-bye, and just let them go. Business will thrive once you do.

4. **INVEST IN YOURSELF BEFORE YOU EXPECT OTHERS TO INVEST IN YOU.** Don't worry about finding investors or outside capital until you've invested as much as you can in your business. Do the hard work. Sacrifice. Build your list of fans and potential customers. Create a prototype of your product. Launch your website. Survey potential clients. Don't expect someone else to invest money in your business until you've done all you can to get the ball rolling.

5. **ONLY TAKE CRITICISM IF IT COMES WITH A SOLUTION.** A friend of mine shared a quote with me some years ago. "Effective people starve problems and feed solutions." Everyone has an opinion. Some say they're like . . . well, you know what they say. Not everyone will buy into your vision. Learn to discern what comments or criticisms are worth your time and consideration.

I'm not suggesting you not be teachable or coachable—everyone should be. But I've learned from my own experience that if someone only chooses to point out flaws and failures, without providing examples of how I can fix the problem, then they're not really trying to help me.

HOW CAN I NETWORK EFFECTIVELY?

Your network determines your net worth. Who you will be in five years is directly related to the people you associate with now. Read any book on success, and you'll find a common theme. They all stress the importance of leveraging relationships. Working in teams is an absolute

AFFIRM

I surround myself with intelligent and successful people.

necessity, and attempting to work in solitude is absolutely ludicrous. You need other people, preferably people that are either smarter than you on certain subjects or have more experience than you in some area of life or business.

If you've ever been to a networking event, you've probably run into a few ineffective networkers. Sorry to say it, but you may be one of them, just like I used to be, running around pushing your business card on people without slowing to build a real connection. Or maybe you recognize the standoffish dude who expects everyone to find him in the corner and strike up a conversation.

There are better ways to network, and networking is essential to growing your business, brand, and life. Use these tips to get it done effectively.

1. **BE PREPARED.** Attending a networking event without business cards is a rookie mistake. While the most important thing is showing up, show up as a professional. When you meet your ideal client, partner, or sponsor, what do you think their perception of you will be if you're unprepared? You wouldn't want them to assume you handle business with the same lack of preparedness.

2. **SET GOALS BEFORE YOU WALK IN.** Know what you're looking for before you even enter the event. Are you on the hunt for a new job? Are you looking for partnerships, clients, or investors? How about a professional in a complementary industry? Of course, you should stay open to all kinds of possibilities, but there's nothing wrong with knowing what you want beforehand. Then you can make sure that your conversations are focused and intentional, which is important when time is limited.

3. **ARRIVE ON TIME.** Most networking opportunities take place first thing in the morning, during lunch hour, or immediately after work. Think about these timeframes. Most people will have to rush off some place and won't have time to linger. Either they're scurrying to work in the morning, back to work in the afternoon, or home to care for families in the evening. If you want to have the greatest chance to meet the most people, you need to be there during the peak time, which is the one hour smack dab in the middle. But arrive earlier if you want to take advantage of free food. No one wants to get to know you while you're stuffing your face!

4. **GET YOUR ELEVATOR SPEECH TIGHT.** Be able to intelligently articulate what you do, who you do it for, and two or three benefits you can provide for your ideal clients—in ninety seconds or less. If you're talking for two or three minutes about what you do, you're probably well into ramble mode, and you may have lost the interest of whoever is listening.

Be ready to articulate what you do and who you do it for in ninety seconds or less.

As an example, an elevator speech for Dr. Phil of television fame might sound like this. "My name is Dr. Phil, and I'm a licensed therapist who helps families reconnect, rebuild, and reaffirm their love for one another. Who do you know who might need my services?"

Write down a few different versions of your elevator speech, practice them in the mirror, and memorize them. Don't forget to ask for the sale, if the person you're talking to seems like a fit for your service or product, or ask for a referral to a friend or colleague who might be interested. When your elevator speech is really tight, people will begin to self-select and ask to work with you before you even get around to asking for their business.

5. **WORK THE CROWD.** This is probably the one that most people struggle with the most. Once we find people we like, we can ride out the entire night with them and feel über-successful at the end of the event. But by not mingling, you'll miss the opportunity to meet many more wonderful people and to make important contacts. Some networking pros suggest that you spend no more than six to eight minutes with a person. This is enough time to determine whether there's a connection and to be polite when ending the conversation. Time yourself and be ready to close with something like "Pleasure meeting you, but I have to make my rounds. I'll email you by X."

6. **KEEP THINGS PROFESSIONAL.** Regardless of where the event is held, remember this is business. You may be in a club setting with alcohol flowing, but don't let it confuse your sensibilities. Any event branded as "networking" should be considered just that. This isn't about socializing, and it certainly isn't the time for you to pick up anyone or be picked up by anyone. As a matter of fact, I'd have suspicions about any woman

looking for a man at a networking event. If something blossoms between you, won't you wonder what's really going on when she's out
networking every week? But I digress. At the end of the day, no sugges-
tive dancing, foul language of any kind, or excessive drinking.

7. **FOLLOW UP QUICKLY.** You can follow each of the previous steps to a tee,
    but the introduction is just the beginning. If you don't work on build-
    ing the relationship within three days of making the acquaintance, the
    likelihood that you'll create something lasting decreases drastically.
    You may not want to have a follow-up meeting with every person you
    meet, but at least connect with these people on LinkedIn. If you have
    a well-manicured page, they can learn more about you than you could
    have expressed in six to eight minutes. Identify your top three contacts
    from the event and send a genuine email that suggests some type of
    further communication within the next two weeks. Build a relation-
    ship, keeping in mind that people do business with people they like.

YOU ARE YOUR BEST INVESTMENT

CONTINUALLY WORKING ON YOUR personal and professional development isn't about spending more money. It's about investing in both your mental growth and future income. Continuous learning is a wealthy habit. Wealthy people recognize that our careers, businesses, and personal endeavors cannot possibly grow when we settle in a fixed mindset that limits our thinking and requires us to rely solely on status, ego, or past experience in a world continuously faced with new innovations and new challenges. When you fail to nurture your mindset and skill set in order to embrace these challenges, you accept failure before the opportunity to succeed ever presents itself.

Whether it's the books you buy, the seminars, conferences, and trainings you choose to attend, or even the coaches or mentors you hire, education and personal advancement on any and every level is the secret weapon of the wealthy, powerful, and successful. In the words of Jim Rohn, a self-made millionaire famous for sharing his own rags to riches story, "Formal education will make you a living; self-education will make you a fortune."

Rarely is business success attributed to never having failed or to having the good fortune to avoid setbacks. Quite the contrary. A common theme you'll find from studying the courageous men and women who've triumphed

AFFIRM

I benefit often from seeking wise counsel.

in the business world is that their investment in self-education ensured that, no matter what happened, they always had the attitude and mindset to stand back up, dust themselves off, and create their empires again.

You must understand beyond a shadow of a doubt that what you nurture grows. The investment you make in your personal and professional growth and development is the one thing that no unfortunate circumstance or ill-intentioned person can ever take away from you. You are your best investment!

HOW CAN I AFFORD PERSONAL AND PROFESSIONAL DEVELOPMENT WHEN I'M BROKE?

Personal and professional development both come in many forms. Your willingness to seek them out depends on whether you truly see the ongoing acquisition of knowledge as an investment in your future or not. Those who practice non-wealthy habits will rarely see a workshop, seminar, or online coaching series as something that will pay off more than its cost, but they'll jump at an opportunity to wield the term "investment" when it comes to depreciating items like a luxury car or a name brand television. In essence, non-wealthy people tend to view objects as investments. Successful people invest in continuous learning. No matter what risks they take, if they lose it all, no one can steal their knowledge. The question isn't really *if* you can afford to invest in personal and professional development. The question is how can you afford not to?

Real MONEY
Investment in education and professional development is the secret weapon of the wealthy, powerful, and successful.

Don't limit yourself with the belief that continuous learning requires you to shell out thousands of dollars. There are hundreds of programs that offer no-cost and low-cost education in the areas of financial literacy, small business development, marketing, the arts, and much more. This journey is about the mindset. When you approach your ongoing education as though everything costs too much, or there aren't any programs out there, then you're absolutely right. It is too expensive, and there aren't any good programs out there for *you*. Meanwhile, someone who fits your exact profile in your very own city is taking advantage of all types of programming that will help get his life on track. Everything begins with a decision. You, and only you, have the power to decide whether your glass will be half empty or half full.

If your glass is, in fact, half full, follow these low-cost or no-cost tips to get started on your personal and professional development path today.

1. **GET YOUR MIND RIGHT, AND START WHERE YOU ARE.** Once you've wrapped your mind around the fact that you can and should move forward on this path, identify what area you want to improve first and commit to starting where you are. Your first target area may be finances, branding, marketing, relationships, fitness, health, spirituality, parenting, or any number of subjects. The beauty is that as you push yourself to grow, the Universe will continue to bring forth amazing opportunities. Just commit to beginning today.

2. **READ FOR AN HOUR OR MORE PER DAY.** A 2012 study by the Nielsen Company found that the average American household spends over five hours per day watching television. This translates to nine years of life spent sitting in front of a box. Imagine how much further along you'll be than the average person if you make a conscious decision to use some of that time to read, rather than allowing your brain to slip into a semi-comatose state for hours each day.

UN
REAL

The average American spends over five hours per day watching TV-- time that could be spent learning.

3. **INCORPORATE LEARNING INTO YOUR NORMAL ROUTINE.** Check out books on audio from the local library or download a few on your mobile device. You can listen while getting dressed in the morning, cleaning the house, working out at the gym, or on the go. Some of my clients use their long commutes to work as an opportunity for school on wheels. Instead of wasting time on Facebook while you're waiting for an appointment, carry something you can pull out and read. The point is to make this a part of your lifestyle, as opposed to claiming you don't have time to read.

4. **TAKE ADVANTAGE OF FREE OPPORTUNITIES TO LEARN.** Don't ignore every late-night infomercial. Some offer tickets to complimentary half-day seminars.

Don't go with an attitude of defensiveness because you expect some-one to try to sell you something. While you may be 110% right about that, you set the rules for how that game is played in your world. Go with the understanding that you want to learn at least one new concept and have an opportunity to network with new people. If you're truly not interested in what's for sale, don't feel pressured to buy anything. Simply take your notes home, determine what you can and cannot use, implement immediately, and move on.

5. **FIND A MENTOR.** Your success in any area of life is strongly determined by the people in your life. Not only do you require the support and en-couragement of others to make meaningful progress, but you'll often find yourself leaning on them for advice. My personal rule of thumb in this area is to not take advice from someone who isn't where I want to be or has never been where I'm going. Look to mentors who are willing to be transparent about their triumphs and failures to help you navi-gate your course just a little better.

6. **GET A COACH.** A coach will work with you for a specified period of time to help you improve your efficiency and effectiveness in running your own business or in performing your current role within a larger com-pany. Some coaches specialize in specific aspects of business or career development and others take a broader approach. Either way, he or she will analyze your performance, skills, behavior, and attitude to identify specific opportunities for improvement. A good coach will help you put measurable goals in place and walk your through steps to meet those goals.

7. **MASTERMIND GROUPS.** Mastermind groups offer a combination of brain-storming, education, peer support, and accountability in a group setting to help you sharpen your business and personal skills. A mastermind group can only function effectively with commitment, confidentiality, and consistent participation from all members. Search online or reach out to peers to find mastermind groups in your area, or start your own group. There's plenty of information online to direct you in setting up guidelines for a mastermind group that benefits all members.

8. **FIND AN ACCOUNTABILITY PARTNER.** Accountability partners work together to help each other stay on track and reach their goals. Find someone dependable, who will be willing to push you to get specific in your goal setting, and who doesn't mind giving you a swift kick in the rear when you need it. Set up regular check-in times, and consider adding a little friendly competition, like requiring the person who drops the ball in pursuit of his goals to treat his partner to dinner.

I'VE TRIED LOTS OF PROGRAMS FOR PERSONAL AND PROFESSIONAL DEVELOPMENT. WHY HASN'T ANYTHING WORKED?

As a person who offers self-study programs, I'll be the first to tell you there's nothing healthy or cost-effective about being a program junkie. When people ask me what the difference is between other personal finance authorities and me, I describe what I think is different, but then I politely ask them to go back and work through whatever system they've already started. We all have a common goal of helping people lead financially fit lives, and we essentially teach variations of the same information. Who you choose to work with really comes down to a personal preference.

Many people hop around from program to program and system to system searching for a magic bullet to change their lives in seven days or less. I'm honestly amazed at how many people spend ten, twenty, or thirty years running their finances into the ground and then come to me for coaching and expect to see miraculous improvement over night. It's like people who try a ninety-day "get lean" program and quit after three days because they don't see their six-pack developing.

AFFIRM

I always have time to learn new wealth principles.

In truth, many people aren't willing to fully implement the programs they invest in. The creators of good programs structure their material in specific ways to give you the blueprint for how they achieved success in certain areas or how they've helped clients succeed. You can choose the bits and pieces that you really need and ignore areas that perhaps don't pertain to you, but you cannot ignore the entire system or fundamental parts of the system and then say the program doesn't work.

The disclaimers on fitness or business infomercials usually state that the testimonials are from real people, but they're not average results. You know why? It's not because the system or program fails most people. It's because the average person fails to work the system, no matter how much they claim they want the results.

To make progress using any program you've purchased in the last few years, I encourage you to go back through the steps and commit to intense and focused implementation for a designated, thoughtful, reasonable period of time. If the instructions are to give it ninety days, be willing to invest ninety days before taking to online reviews to bash the system. If you can't make the commitment, just accept that the program hasn't worked because you haven't been willing to work it.

SHOULD I GO BACK TO SCHOOL IF I ALREADY HAVE DEBT?

Since the Great Recession started in 2008, many people have used our weakened economy as an opportunity to go back to school and secure advanced degrees. I can see why someone may think this is a viable route to get to the next level of career success during difficult economic times. But this method isn't for everyone. Many people could reach the next level in their careers by simply investing more time in their basic personal and professional development and implementing what they've already learned.

If you plan to go back to school, be clear about your objectives and the odds of those things materializing. For example, I've met people who took out $80,000 to earn an MBA, but years after completion, aren't making any more money than they were before they got the extra degree. Adding letters behind your name or seeing your name embossed in gold on a fancy certificate may feel great, but paying back nearly a hundred grand in loans won't feel so good if you're not earning significantly more money.

If your current employer offers some type of higher education incentive, then by all means, take advantage of it, if you're convinced that getting the additional degree will make the impact you want. As with any endeavor, the ultimate results are based upon how much work you're willing to put in after the classes have ended.

Beware of the bucket list mentality. "I'm just doing it because I've always wanted to," isn't a good reason to go into debt. While I'm a fan of accomplishing whatever you set your mind to, I'm not a fan of adding additional debt to your life simply because the experience somehow makes you happy.

Are there instances when going back to school, with or without taking on debt, has helped someone advance personally and professionally? Of course. But I find that those people usually create a solid plan before embarking upon the educational journey. They've researched, spoken to mentors, found the cheapest route to accomplish their goal, and planned what they'll do with the new knowledge. More than likely, these are people who haven't decided to go back to school simply to live off of a refund check, which sadly happens quite frequently. They've put in the work to make it work and obtain the results many hope for, but few achieve.

IS IT POSSIBLE TO AVOID STUDENT LOANS IF I GO BACK TO SCHOOL?

As an adult in the real world, you've learned by now that the notion of going to school, taking out more loans than you can afford, and banking on getting a high-paying job at the end of it all is completely delusional. With living expenses, the average cost of a graduate program at a public university is about $30,000 per year and rising, with private colleges costing about 30% more. Undergraduate tuition isn't far behind. With this in mind, you should definitely be concerned about what it will take to make it through with minimal debt and the smallest amount of money out of pocket.

UN REAL

The average cost of graduate school at a public university is $30,000 per year and rising.

It's possible to avoid student loans, whether your desire is to complete your undergraduate degree or return as a graduate student. No different than the advice given to high school students and their parents, it all comes down to whether or not you plan properly and plan well enough in advance.

Here are a few ways you can avoid student loans.

Real MONEY

Scholarships, fellowships, and assistantships should be the first options you explore to finance a degree.

9. **EXPLORE SCHOLARSHIPS, FELLOWSHIPS, AND ASSISTANTSHIPS.** Undergraduate schools generally have a central financial aid office, where you can get information about aid for any degree program. In many graduate programs, aid is given out by academic departments or the specific graduate school instead of the central financial aid office. In that case, you should search for a graduate admissions official or someone affiliated with the program to help you sort through available options.

10. **ENTICE SCHOOLS TO COMPETE FOR YOU.** If you happened to be a top student in your undergraduate studies, apply to several graduate schools and let them know you're searching for the best financial aid package. They might compete with a strong offer in order to convince you to choose their school.

11. **GET YOUR CURRENT EMPLOYER TO PAY.** Approximately 50% of U.S. companies have some type of tuition assistance program in place. Many companies looking to boost their collective skill set, without hiring new people and spending resources on training, will sponsor all or part of an employee's graduate schooling through tuition reimbursement. If your company doesn't, talk with the human resources department about how a master's degree or Ph.D. would benefit both you and the company. Emphasize the connection between your coursework and your job description.

> **Real MONEY**
> About 50% of U.S. companies offer some type of tuition assistance to employees.

Having your education paid for by your employer might mean committing to work for the company for a set period after you complete the degree or program. If you leave the company early, you may have to pay back part of the tuition.

12. **RESEARCH POTENTIAL TAX BENEFITS.** There are three different ways to take advantage of tax benefits for graduate school: the Lifetime Learning Tax Credit, tuition expense deductions, and student loan interest deductions.

Ask your tax professional to make sure you take advantage of these methods which allows individuals to subtract thousands of dollars annually from their tax bill.

13. **TALK TO YOUR UNDERGRADUATE SCHOOL.** If they have a graduate program, many schools will offer a tuition discount to alumni. This is especially true if you finished with great undergraduate grades and can snag a few recommendation letters from respected professors who are still there.

MANAGE MONEY WISELY

"Without self-discipline, success is impossible, period." – Lou Holtz

EARLIER IN THIS BOOK, I cite the case of Mike Tyson, who earned hundreds of millions of dollars but lost it all, eventually filing bankruptcy. Sadly, he's one of a long list of professional athletes—including Latrell Sprewell, Lawrence "L.T." Taylor, Mark Brunell, and Scottie Pippen—who earn the kind of money most of us can only dream of, only to end up seeking relief in bankruptcy court because their debts outweigh their assets. In fact, an analysis by *Sports Illustrated* in 2009 found that 60% of NBA athletes were broke within five years of retiring. Football players fared even worse, with 78% of NFL athletes bankrupt or struggling financially within just two years of retirement.

Don't just skim over those statistics. Take them in and understand that the majority of the people you watch running up and down a field or a court will end up no better off financially—and in many cases, worse off—than the average American. Why? Most of them don't come from backgrounds that taught them a lot about personal finance. They never learn how to wisely manage all the cash rolling in, so they can't hold on to it.

It doesn't matter how much you earn if you don't know what to do with your money. When you're struggling to make ends meet, it's easy to tell yourself, "If only I made more money, I'd be fine." But financial success isn't based solely on income. Take the example of Joseph Leek. An insurance salesman born in Great Britain in 1912, he never earned a remarkable salary. Leek lived in a modest home and bought his clothes secondhand. By all appearances he didn't have much in the way of material success, but over his lifetime, he quietly amassed a fortune by investing his money in the stock market. When he died in 2003 at the age of ninety, Joseph Leek left $1.8 million to charity.

Being a good steward over your finances means taking care of, and showing respect for, what you have now. If you can't manage $100 wisely, then why on earth would the Universe trust you with $100,000? If it did, consciously or subconsciously, you'd likely find a way to mismanage it. To make the most of what you earn over the long term, decide today that you're ready to manage money wisely.

GET IT TOGETHER!

IT'S EASY TO CLAIM you want to save more, invest more, and become debt-free, but with the wrong advice and no money management system in place, even the greatest of intentions go to waste.

The first step in managing your money wisely is to show respect for the money you already have. Checking your mailbox less than once a month and leaving receipts in the console of your car aren't signs of respect. A sign of respect is utilizing a money-managing method that's easy for you to maintain, an organized system rather than a shoebox under your bed. De-cluttering and organizing financial records is your first opportunity to not only remove the physical clutter, but to also clear away the mental clutter that consumes your ability to manage money effectively. After all, it's difficult to get your financial life in order when your financial documents are completely out of order!

It's equally difficult to get your finances in order when you're getting no financial advice at all, or even worse, bad advice from people who don't know what they're talking about. With a few simple steps, you can build a financial team and implement a system, both of which will help you reach your goals.

WHAT DOCUMENTS SHOULD EVERY MAN HAVE ON HAND?

It's easy to think of financial documents as nothing more than a few utility statements and sales receipts, but for a complete picture, you'll need to pull together much more. So get what you can find out of shoeboxes, off your kitchen counter, out of junk drawers or the little envelopes with months printed on them, or wherever you've been cramming all the bills, check stubs, and other stuff you swore you'd organize one day. Today's the day.

Real TALK

Removing the physical clutter will clear away the mental clutter and allow you to manage your money effectively.

Review the list of important documents below, gather them together, and indicate whether you (H) have the document, (N) need to obtain the document, or (X) the document doesn't apply to your household.

Collect the documents you have, and request the ones you need. This process sets the foundation for you to work through the rest of this section of the book.

CHECKLIST OF IMPORTANT
LEGAL DOCUMENTS & FINANCIAL STATEMENTS

Important Legal Documents that Apply to My Family

_____ 1. Birth Certificate(s)/Adoption Papers

_____ 2. Marriage License

_____ 3. Divorce Papers

_____ 4. Social Security Card(s)

_____ 5. Passport/Green Card(s)

_____ 6. Naturalization Documents

_____ 7. Will

_____ 8. Power(s) of Attorney (Personal/Property)

_____ 9. Mortgage or Real Estate Deeds of Trust

_____ 10. Vehicle Registration/Ownership

_____ 11. Other

Tax Statements

_____ 12. Previous 3 Years' Tax Returns

_____ 13. Property Tax Statements

_____ 14. Personal Property Tax Statements

_____ 15. Other

Financial Accounts

_____ 16. Bank/Credit Union Statements

_____ 17. Credit/Debit Card Statements

_____ 18. Retirement Accounts (401K, TSP, IRA, etc.)

_____ 19. Investment Accounts (Stocks, Bonds, Mutual Funds, etc.)

_____ 20. Other

Sources of Income/Assets

_____ 21. Recent Pay Stubs for All Sources of Income

_____ 22. Government Benefits (Social Security, Temporary Assistance for Needy Families, Veterans', etc.)

_____ 23. Alimony Income

_____ 24. Child Support Income

_____ 25. Professional Appraisals of Personal Property

_____ 26. Rewards Accounts (Frequent Flyer Programs, Hotel Rewards, etc.)

_____ 27. Other

Financial Obligations

_____ 28. Mortgage Statements

_____ 29. Lease

_____ 30. Utility Bills (Electric, Water, Gas)

_____ 31. Car Payments

_____ 32. Student Loans

_____ 33. Alimony Payments

_____ 34. Child Support Payments

_____ 35. Elder Care Facilities

_____ 36. Other Debts

Insurance

_____ 37. Property Insurance

_____ 38. Rental Insurance

_____ 39. Auto Insurance

_____ 40. Life Insurance

_____ 41. Other

Medical

_____ 42. Health Insurance ID Card(s)

_____ 43. Record of Immunizations/Allergies

_____ 44. List of Necessary Medications

_____ 45. Disabilities Documentation

_____ 46. Living Will

_____ 47. Dental Records/Child Identity Cards/DNA records

_____ 48. Other

Military

_____ 49. Current Military ID

_____ 50. Military Discharge DD 214

_____ 51. Other

Other Financial/Legal Documentation

_____ 52. _____

_____ 53. _____

_____ 54. _____

Once you have all of these documents together, make a copy of the entire packet. Important information is often printed on the back side of these documents, so please be sure to copy both sides. Store the document copies in a safe deposit box or a small waterproof and fireproof safe, which you can find at office supply stores.

*Download Operation HOPE's Emergency Financial First Aid Kit to print down the entire checklist as well as other Personal Household Information worksheets by visiting http://www.operationhope.org/emergency-kit

HOW CAN I KEEP MY FINANCES ORGANIZED?

In the last exercise, you found all of your most important legal documents and financial statements. (See: *What documents should every man have on hand?*) It's time to organize them in a systematic way that will save you from ever having your important information in disarray again.

My financial life is in order, because my financial documents are in order.

This is a great exercise to do with your significant other. You want to build a financially successful family, so making sure you're both aware of what you have and where you keep it is an important step in the right direction.

WHAT'S NEEDED
     1 Dozen Hanging File Folders
     1 Box of 25 File Folders
     1 Plastic File Tote

WHAT TO DO

STEP ONE:
Label the first hanging file folder **"Legal Documents."** In it, place items that are imperative to keep track of, but which don't necessarily fall into a financial category. In one folder, you'll place vital records like birth certificates and adoption papers. In another, you might place your marriage license or divorce decree. Here is where you'll also file your social security card, passport, and green card or naturalization documents. Copies of wills and powers of attorney, in sealed envelopes, should also be placed here.

STEP TWO:
Label the second hanging file folder **"Tax Returns."** In it, place three file folders, one for last year, the present year, and next year. Mark the year on each folder's tab, and put into it all of that year's important tax documents, like W-2 forms or 1099s. If you can't find the documents, but used professional tax preparers in the past, call them and ask for back copies.

STEP THREE:
Label the third hanging folder **"Financial Accounts."** If you have several checking and savings accounts, create separate file folders for each of them. Keep your monthly bank statements here, as well as any ATM slips or deposit slips you retrieve during the month. (Note: If you have several accounts with no money in them, just consolidate. Don't waste time, energy, or paper.) Additionally, use this area to store information about retirement accounts (401k, TSP, IRA, etc.) and investment accounts (stocks, bonds, mutual funds, etc.).

STEP FOUR:
Label the fourth hanging folder **"Income and Assets."** Create a folder to store recent paystubs or copies of checks received for self-employment income. Hold on to proof of all government benefits such as social security income. Use a separate folder if you receive or pay alimony or child support.

Compare billing statements, such as cable and phone bills, over a period of time to catch any billing errors.

STEP FIVE:
Label the fifth hanging folder **"Household."** If you're a homeowner, this includes mortgage statements, property tax bills, HOA documents, and other related expenses. If you're a renter, this should contain your lease, the receipt for your security deposit, renter's insurance policy, and the receipts for your rental payments. I would also include folders for electricity, gas, and cable, and other recurring household expenses. You should keep up with these regularly too. My clients have caught hundreds of dollars erroneously charged on phone and cable bills by comparing multiple statements over a period of time. Don't forget to also include any agreements you have between yourself and any roommates or boarders, relationships which have become rather common since the Great Recession. No matter how close you are as friends, when money is involved, document everything!

STEP SIX:
Label the sixth hanging folder **"Credit Card DEBT."** Make sure to capitalize the word DEBT, so it stands out and bothers you every time you see it. I'm not kidding. Create a separate file for each credit card account you

have. Prayerfully, this step does not take up all your file folders. If it does, no worries. We'll handle that shortly.

STEP SEVEN:
Label the seventh hanging folder **"Loans."** Place any documents associated with your loans here. This may include student loans, car loans, personal loans, and the like. Each debt should have its own folder, so Sallie Mae has one folder, and your Chase Student loan has another. Each folder should contain the loan note, your statements, and payment records.

STEP EIGHT:
Label the eighth hanging folder **"Insurance."** It will contain separate folders for each of your insurance policies, which may include car insurance, health insurance, disability insurance, and the like. Remember your homeowner's or renter's policies should have been filed away in the Household section. If you have any other policies besides those, include them here as well.

STEP NINE:
If you have children, put together a folder labeled **"Children's Documents."** It should hold all statements and other records pertaining to any accounts they have and accounts you have for them, such as college savings. I also add a folder for child care to keep track of those expenses for tax purposes, as well as a folder with immunization records and other health-related documents needed for school.

STEP TEN:
Label the tenth hanging folder **"Personal."** It should contain files for personal expenses such as clothing, grooming, dental services, organization dues, and the like. Create a specific folder for your medical files, such as copies of your health insurance cards, statements from your physician's office or the hospital, and lists of necessary medications.

As you begin the process of putting together your system, you may find you're missing some documents. Whatever the reason you don't have them on hand, today is a new day. That was something the old you didn't keep up with, because no one taught you how much it could simplify your life.

Now that you know better, put the files together as best you can, and figure out how or where to get your hands on whatever's missing. The important thing is that you've taken the first step, and that's something you should definitely be proud of!

HOW LONG SHOULD I KEEP FINANCIAL DOCUMENTS?

Consistently managing your money can create a lot of paperwork. Once you have your filing system in place, shred documents periodically to make sure you always have the most recent and relevant information. (See: *How can I keep my finances organized?*) Don't burden yourself by keeping these documents longer than necessary.

If you're like me and prefer to have things on hand longer, scan the documents before you shred them. Save the scanned images in organized folders on your computer, but remember to back it up often.

If you opt for paperless or e-billing and receive your statements in your e-mail box, there's no need to scan. You can simply save each statement as a PDF. It saves time, paper, and energy, but make sure it's the right choice for you. Will you open and review the statement or bill the same way you would if it arrived on paper? It's easy to forget about bills that only exist on the Internet.

Here are some timeframes for keeping financial records.

KEEP FOR A YEAR OR LESS:
- **Monthly Bills** – Review for accuracy, but there's no need to keep them for more than a quarter at the most.
- **Credit Card Bills** – Review for any billing errors, and keep for at least six months.
- **Paycheck Stubs** – You should always have your last three pay stubs.

  You never know when you'll need to prove income for a loan or some other necessity. Keep the last few in the year to compare against your W-2 or 1099. If they don't match, go to your employer and request a correction. Otherwise, you can shred them. Your W-2 is sufficient for filing taxes.
- **Insurance Policies** – Always keep the most recent policy. Old ones don't matter once a new one takes effect.

KEEP FOR TWO YEARS:

- **Bank Statements** – Review statements when you receive them. Look for unauthorized purchases, and keep twenty-four months of statements on hand. For the self-employed, this is particularly important. In some instances, the absence of a regular W-2 and paycheck stubs means you'll need to prove your income by using bank statements.

KEEP FOR SEVEN YEARS:

- **Tax Documents** – I know seven years seems like forever, but so will an IRS audit, if you don't have your tax returns in order. If you think you're due a larger refund, you have three years to file an amended return, and the IRS has three years to audit you, if they think you made a mistake. The IRS has six years to audit you when they think you underreported income, and there's no time limit when they believe you blatantly filed a fraudulent return.

    If you've lost old tax returns and would feel better if you had a copy, contact your tax preparer, and if all else fails, request a copy of past tax returns from the IRS. You can get a tax return transcript for free in about two weeks by calling 1-800-829-1040.

KEEP FOREVER OR INDEFINITELY:

- **Loan Documents** – Keep these for the life of the loan, and destroy them once you've paid them off and have a title or other final document proving payment in full.
- **Receipts** – Keep anything documenting a major purchase, like jewelry or a computer. You never know when it might come in handy.
- **Long-term insurance policies or investment accounts** – Keep these documents until maturation of the investment.
- **Brokerage Statements** – If you've already begun investing, you'll get monthly statements telling you how much you've made each month. Keep brokerage statements until you receive the annual statement at the end of each year. Keep annual statements until you sell the investment. You'll use the statements to prove your capital gains or losses when you file taxes.

WHAT SOFTWARE DO YOU SUGGEST FOR MANAGING MONEY EFFECTIVELY?

New money-management software options hit the market all the time, and there's no one-size-fits-all, perfect program. You can expect to find options that allow you to manage every aspect of your finances, including your accounts, bills, investments, taxes, planning, and goal setting. I prefer web-based programs, because they're consistently updated. These can cost up to $19.99 per month, but you can also find free options.

The ideal personal finance software for you should be based on your personal money style, give basic advice to help you make informed decisions, and provide ample user-friendly features. It should make managing your finances convenient and stress-free, identify money leaks for you, and help you make better investments and increase your personal net worth.

Here's a list of the criteria to search for when choosing personal finance software.

BANKING & BILLS
The ability to import all account data, including transactions, directly into the software is a standard tool you'll need to make wise money decisions. The best personal finance software allows you to manage your savings and checking accounts, as well as your loans, credit cards, and mortgage accounts, in one place.

PERSONAL INVESTING & GOAL SETTING
Look for personal finance software that provides its users with the tools needed to manage stocks, bonds, mutual funds, 401K accounts, and the like. Personal investment options within the software will also allow you to plan for retirement, home purchases, college expenses, debt relief, and other financial goals.

TAX OPTIONS
Some personal finance software can export all of your financial information into tax software, help you find missed deductions, and estimate your tax withholdings and capital gains.

USER FRIENDLINESS
Personal finance software must be extremely easy to use, allowing you to track transactions, set up accounts, and see detailed reports.

REPORTING
Reports are a great way to track your progress. You want to see how well, or not so well, you've done with your money management in any given period of weeks, months, or years. Typical software utilizes pie charts and line graphs to illustrate cash flow, personal investing, and all additional transactions. Seeing exactly where your money is going is essential when you're trying to decide where to cut back in order to save.

HELP & SUPPORT
Search for software that provides an online user manual, customer forum, email support system, and integrated help section.

ARCHIVING & SECURITY
Security is an extremely important feature for your personal finance software. Your account numbers, personal information, and other bank information are used to set up and manage accounts within the software for your convenience.

Having archived financial files saved and categorized is perfect for tax season, or if, by chance, you happen to be audited.

WHAT PROFESSIONALS SHOULD I HAVE ON MY FINANCIAL TEAM?

Your success, in any area of life, is strongly determined by the people with whom you surround yourself. You require the support and encouragement of others to make meaningful progress, but you'll often find yourself leaning on them for advice. And as much as you may love and appreciate close friends and family, you simply can't take financial advice from everyone.

There are several pieces of the financial puzzle that require professional help. Having

Real TALK

The right team of professionals can make sure your money is working for you, not against you.

the right team in place can make all the difference in how you manage your finances and put your money to work for you, instead of against you. Here's a list of the small group of professionals you may need to enlist to advise you on business and personal finance decisions.

PERSONAL FINANCE COACH - I'm not starting with a personal finance coach simply to toot my own horn. Quite often I receive referrals from colleagues in other financial disciplines who wish their clients had met with someone like me first. It's very difficult for a financial planner or advisor to do their job when the client lacks basic budgeting skill, claims he can't find the money to save, and is still struggling with a sense that he needs to provide for his extended family at his own detriment. These professionals want to work on more complex investment strategies and long-term planning. If you're starting from scratch and need someone to hold your hand through the process, you should start with a coach that can help you set the foundation and make life easier for the professionals up ahead.

ACCOUNTANT - When life isn't too complicated, and you can file a simple return via TurboTax or one of the other tax preparation software programs, I'm not opposed to that option. But an actual accountant can do a lot more than prepare tax returns. Some will help analyze your big picture and help you set up a system for managing and reviewing your finances. They can also keep pace with life changes that affect your taxes, such as getting married or divorced, having a new child, or sending one off to college. The IRS doesn't care about what you didn't know when an audit hits, so get the advice you need upfront.

Getting your estate in order for the loved ones you'll eventually leave behind should be a top priority.

ESTATE-PLANNING ATTORNEY - While not the most exciting thing to think about, getting things in order to care for the loved ones you'll eventually leave behind needs to be at the top of your priority list. This professional will help assemble the documents necessary to ensure things go smoothly when that inevitable time comes. These documents include a will, financial and medical powers of attorney, which let others make important decisions for you when you can't make them for yourself, and in some cases, a revocable living trust, which lets your estate avoid probate. You may need other documents, dependent upon your unique scenario. You can also do all this for yourself on sites like www.legalzoom.com or www.rocketlawyer.com, but any legal documents should still be reviewed by a professional for accuracy.

FINANCIAL PLANNER - A financial planner helps you create a road map for your financial future. The planner works with you to create plans for retirement, taxes, and college tuition, according to your specific needs and financial objectives for every phase of your adult life. By keeping abreast of new tax laws, current trends, and market developments, a planner works with you on a strategic level.

FINANCIAL ADVISOR - Financial advisors are commonly confused with financial planners. Most people use the titles interchangeably, which is very misleading. Financial advisors deal specifically with investing. Their job is to advise you on how to best invest your money in accordance with the road map you created with your financial planner. The advisor's primary function is to provide guidance. For example, an advisor might guide you in finding the most tax-effective way to save for your child's education. You can use the expertise of a financial advisor to assist primarily with market related investments. Most advisors are highly knowledgeable in the areas of mutual funds, stocks, and bonds. Some financial advisors specialize in specific investment products. There's some debate about whether it's best to go with a fee-based or a commission-based advisor. My view is that the financial advisor's integrity, expertise, and ability to work well with you are more important factors.

MENTOR - No matter how old you are or what you've accomplished, everyone needs wise counsel, either from someone who has the level of success you desire or from someone who's been there, done that, and will be transparent enough to tell you what mistakes to avoid. Once you've surrounded yourself with a team of the best consultants, coaches, and confidants you can find, put a cherry on top and find a mentor that will help you stay clear of the costly mistakes you'll likely make if left to your own devices.

HOW DO I CHOOSE THE RIGHT PROFESSIONALS FOR MY PERSONAL FINANCE TEAM?

Knowing you need professional help is a wonderful first step, but finding a trusted team that understands your personality and objectives takes work. Admittedly, I've only learned to choose the right people through trial and error. I've lost a lot of time and money relying on information from incompetent people. You know when you're so upset you have to speak very slowly so you don't say totally inappropriate things? Yeah, I was upset like that when we got hit with a five-figure tax bill a few years back.

Real TALK

I lost a lot of time and money relying on advice from people who don't know what they're doing. Find an expert!

When we thought about it more deeply, however, Gerald and I recognized where we went wrong. We didn't have a system for how we evaluated the people who got to be on our team. We were so busy "making moves" that we went with the first referral we received, instead of doing our due diligence. We should have made a change when our life circumstances grew beyond the experience and expertise of our professional. We wanted them to learn what we needed and keep up with our growth, but you need someone who's already an expert at what they do.

When you put together your personal finance team, save yourself some time, money, and heartache with these tips.

1. **EVALUATE YOUR NEEDS, STRENGTHS, AND WEAKNESSES.** While you want to keep a list of strong individuals and companies at your fingertips, you probably won't need everyone all the time. Your team might include an accountant, insurance agent, or financial planner, but you'll only call on each one when the need arises. Know your strengths, and figure out where and when you need help with your weaknesses.

2. **USE REFERRALS.** The best way to find someone reliable is to ask for recommendations from your friends, family, and colleagues who've experienced a high level of care and service and have reaped the benefits you desire. Keep in mind that you're looking for referrals from people with whom you share similar profiles. If you're renting and have

no assets, it's probably not necessary to pay the fees charged by your multi-millionaire uncle's CPA just yet.

3. **ASK FOR A CONSULTATION.** I learned not to wait until the last minute to reach out to new professionals and meet with them one-on-one. Most professionals offer free consultations, but many people don't take them up on it. If you've taken time to evaluate your needs, you should be able to compile a list of questions to ask. This isn't about getting free advice crammed into a twenty-minute session. This is about determining the proper fit for a long-term professional relationship.

Real MONEY

Take advantage of free consultations to ask questions and determine if each professional is the right fit for you.

4. **TRUST YOUR GUT.** Only hire people with whom you feel a connection. Ask yourself how easy it is to talk with the person. If it's easy to talk to him or her about everyday matters—family, background, the economy—you'll find it's easier to talk about business. That doesn't mean you only look for someone you like on a personal level. They still have to be qualified. (Just saying. Unfortunately, I've made that mistake, too.)

5. **FIND SOMEONE WHO THINKS AHEAD.** I've learned to hire people who think like entrepreneurs, as they should, and forecast for themselves and for me. With so much going on, you don't have time for people waiting on you to tell them what to do. Besides, you probably won't even know what needs to be done next. That's why the heck you're hiring professionals! It's valuable to work with folks who can help you avoid potential pitfalls rather than people who help you recover from mistakes.

6. **DON'T FEAR CHANGE.** If a member of your financial team isn't working out, make a substitution before you lose your shirt behind their antics. You may have to try a few people before you find the right one. That's okay. As you move along and adjust your own expectations, you'll eventually find the right fit.

BUDGETING EFFECTIVELY

WE PROBABLY DON'T NEED to cover the many ineffective methods you've discovered for budgeting over the years. Your "system" has probably left you asking yourself questions like:

Didn't I just get paid?
Why am I broke already?
Why is it so hard to stick to a budget?
Shouldn't I have way more money saved by now?
Did I really pay a $34 overdraft fee for a $5 purchase?

At some point, you've got to get tired of working hard, getting paid, and then looking up and wondering where all your money went. The foundation of developing good financial habits rests upon your ability to master budgeting. Before your brows furrow, remember that budgeting is about creating the vision for your money and making it plain. Your budget tells your money where to go, so it's working for you and not against you.

Your budget sets the tone for the rest of your financial plan. How much you can save, give, spend, invest, and pay down debt all hinges on your ability to budget effectively.

WHY DO I REALLY NEED A BUDGET?

Have you ever gotten paid on a Friday and been broke by Monday? Think that's extreme? Not if you ask 30% of the people I teach and coach. It helps to realize a budget is just a tool to help you decide where your money is going. Remember that Habakkuk 2:2 says, "Write the vision and make it plain." A budget is your vision for your money. You're plainly writing down how your money's coming in and determining how it should go out, without trying to keep it all in your head.

Real TALK

Your budget sets the tone for your financial plan and provides the foundation for developing wealthy habits.

Budgeting is also instrumental in determining where the holes are in your financial planning. If you want to save more, invest, or pay off debt, but can't figure out how you can possibly do it all, a budget will help you find the missing money. In the *Mindset + Money Master Class*®, I show participants how finding just $50 in your budget can help cut your debt repayment time in half. I walk you through the process and give you a spreadsheet I've created to let you plug in your own numbers and see how quickly you can reach your goals.

Real TALK

You should run your household finances like a business. Make decisions based on the numbers, not on emotions.

Run your household like a business. Businesses determine when to hire, fire, and make significant purchases based on the budget. Imagine, as the CEO of your life, being able to create logical systems and take calculated steps based on the facts, not the fictional and emotional places from which many of us manage our money.

HOW DO I DIFFERENTIATE BETWEEN NEEDS AND WANTS?

This is one of the most important questions in personal finance. It's also one of the most overlooked. The false perception is that this concept is so simple everyone should have it mastered. In truth, while many people can define the words "need" and "want," it's difficult to assess the difference during the most important times, like when you're surfing the Internet and making impulse buys, or when you set out to create a realistic and effective budget.

What have you heard? That a need is clothing, food, and shelter and a want is *everything* else? That type of answer goes back to the verbal influences we learned about earlier. (See: *What the heck is a financial blueprint anyway?*)

AFFIRM

I am grateful for all the money I possess today.

Because needs and wants are different for different people, and change for the same person at different stages in life, it's impossible to provide a specific and clear-cut list of needs and wants.

I define a "need" as something *absolutely* necessary to your well-being. Does that include clothing, food, and shelter? Yes. But it may also include a cell phone, or Internet connection, or gas for your car, depending on you need to support yourself.

In addition, my definition of a "want" is something you'd prefer to have and which you perceive will make a beneficial impact on your life. Although we can all make great cases for the extras, those wants become detrimental to your financial success when their purchase is impulsive and not planned and saved for within your budget.

Real TALK

A "need" is something absolutely necessary to your well-being. A "want" is something you'd like to have.

If you don't define your financial needs and wants, you're likely to make poor purchasing decisions. Sure, you'll be temporarily satisfied after buying something you wanted. You might also find yourself unable to adequately or effortlessly take care of your needs.

As a personal finance coach, I ask my clients to go deeper than questioning their wants and needs. Before every purchase, I advise them to ask these four guiding questions:

Do I need it?
Do I want it?
Am I making an investment?
Am I just spending money?

When you make an investment in something, you should reasonably expect a return on your investment. When you just spend money, you should reasonably expect to get absolutely nothing in return, except maybe a short-lived warm, tingly feeling and a few compliments from friends. And if you spend the money without hopes of a substantial return, at least make sure you can afford it, so you're not left feeling guilty.

WHY IS BUDGETING SO FREAKIN' HARD?

Real MONEY

To create a budget you can follow, keep it simple and flexible.

Creating a budget is a marvelous first step, but far too often that's where the story ends. Many people give up on budgeting when they find their plan is far too rigid, intimidating, complicated, and restrictive. For a realistic budget you can stick to, focus on the following factors.

1. **ATTITUDE.** First and foremost, your attitude toward creating a budget has to be healthy. If you think that budgets stink, then guess what? Your budgeting experience will stink! My clients learn to call their budgets a "Prosperity Plan" or "Wealth-Building Map." The title doesn't matter, as long as it gets you excited about managing and mastering your money.

2. **PURPOSE.** A budget should have a defined goal you'd like to achieve within a specified time period. The goal will help you focus when discipline feels like deprivation. Once your budget helps you obtain one goal, set another one. Never stop setting specific, achievable goals. Without goals, you'll grow neglectful, and before you know it, you'll let months slide by without thinking of, or looking at, your budget. Don't become complacent when there's always another goal you can be striving to reach.

3. **SIMPLICITY.** The more complicated you make the budgeting process the less likely you are to stick with it. Think about where you are in life and stick with what speaks to you. If you're relatively young, don't have

children, and have minimal assets and debts, don't overwhelm yourself with a budget your parents would use. They may have tons of different income sources, assets, and investments that don't apply to you right now. Cut the unnecessary line items from your document.

4. **FLEXIBILITY.** The budgeting process is designed to be flexible. Recognize up front that your budget will change from month to month and will require at least monthly review. For example, if you go over in one category, then it should be accounted for next month, or you need to plan to prevent that overage. If you increase spending in one area, then some other area must decrease. At no time can you have more outgoing than incoming. If you want to spend more, you need to first figure out a way to earn more. Don't get frustrated. It's basic math.

Before you can spend more, you need to figure out how to earn more.

HOW DO I MAKE A BUDGET THE RIGHT WAY?

A personal budget is a finance plan that allocates future personal income toward expenses, savings, investments, and debt repayment. The idea of a budget is actually quite simple, despite the fact that the word's almost a taboo term in a culture that moronically believes you should have what you want, when you want it, and worry about the consequences once you're face to face with financial loss.

To create a budget, you'll look at your past spending, as well as future income. There are several methods and tools available for creating, using, and adjusting a personal budget. Although I've listed the most basic categories for you to include in your budget, I honestly don't care what version you use, as long as you use one. Just remember keeping it simple will keep it achievable. Use the parts that apply to your life, and toss the rest. The simpler your budget, the better.

SOME ITEMS TO INCLUDE IN YOUR BUDGET:

<u>Income</u>	<u>Expenses</u>
Earned Income (Money You Worked For)	Charitable Giving
Passive Income	Savings
	Mortgage/Rent
	Utilities
	Cell Phone
	Transportation Costs
	Health Insurance and
	Medical Expenses
	Childcare
	Groceries
	Dining Out
	Taxes
	Clothing
	Fuel
	Cable (No, it's not a utility!)

(See Appendix C for a sample budget.)

HOW DO I KNOW IF I'VE CREATED A REALISTIC BUDGET?

Many people will advise you to track your spending for thirty days in order to see where your money's going and use those numbers to find money leaks, cut spending, and create a budget from what's left. I completely disagree with this method.

After working with hundreds of people, I've noticed something. When people are asked to track their spending, they alter their spending habits. When you know you're being monitored, albeit self-monitored most times, you tend to skew your behavior. You don't want to look or feel bad, so you alter your normal habits and settle for living a pseudo-sacrificial lifestyle to get through those few weeks. Folks that don't commit 110% will spend what they want, lie to themselves, and write down what they think looks good. If this is what you're using to set the foundation for your personal finance success, then your entire budgeting

Real TALK

The truth about your spending behavior is found in your bank statements.

process is doomed! It's based on unrealistic numbers that don't depict your true habits and desired lifestyle. It likely includes numbers pulled out of the sky, or numbers based on what you think they should be, as opposed to what they really are.

realistic |rēə'listik| adjective
1. having or showing a sensible and practical idea of what can be achieved or expected.
2. representing familiar things in a way that is accurate or true to life.

A realistic budget is based on a sensible and practical idea of what can be expected in your behavior, not behavior you've subconsciously altered to feel better about yourself. To find the clearest picture about what's accurate in your spending behavior, examine what you've done already. The recent past is the best indicator of

Real MONEY

To create a realistic budget, use averages from your last three months of bank statements.

future behavior, and the past is rooted in your bank statements. It's based on who you really are and what you actually do—not how you want to look.

Now that your documents are in order, you can gather your last three months of bank statements and use them to create an average dollar amount of how much you spend in each budget category. These numbers will tell you what areas deserve your attention and where to begin your process of realistic budgeting.

CAN YOU EXPLAIN THE CONCEPT OF LIVING BY PERCENTAGES?

Once you've started on the journey toward a realistic budget for your household, you may logically wonder whether or not the amounts you've set are reasonable. Assuming you don't want to be back in the same overspending predicament you were in before, you'll want to include budgeting percentages, an important tool most people leave out.

Real TALK

Too often we try to get what we want and figure out how to pay for it later, rather than choosing to get what we can afford.

Living by percentages isn't difficult to understand, but it's very difficult for many people to implement. We like to get what we want, when we want it, and figure out how to pay for it later, as opposed to choosing what we get based upon what we can actually afford.

AFFIRM

I manage my cents just as much as my dollars.

While there are no exact formulas for figuring out what you should spend in each budget category, experts have come up with percentage guidelines. They're helpful, but keep in mind that adjustments may be necessary for larger family sizes, ages of children, your age, your area's cost of living, the length of your commute, and other factors specific to your lifestyle. These are simply guidelines. At the end of the day, you want your spending to add up to 100%.

Here's a list of what I suggest you spend in each category. Personal finance is never a one-size-fits-all journey. Adjust based on your situation.

Category	Suggested % of Overall Spending
Savings/Investments	10 – 15%
Charitable Giving	10 – 15%
Housing	25 – 30%
Utilities	5 – 10%
Food	10 – 15%
Transportation	10 – 15%
Healthcare	5 – 10%
Debt Payments	5 – 10%
Entertainment/Recreation	5 – 10%
Miscellaneous	5%

Real MONEY

Don't include one-time income in your budget. Using misleading numbers makes it impossible to plan properly.

WHAT IF I HAVE INCONSISTENT INCOME?

Budgeting an irregular income is trickier, but it's not an impossible task. Although your income may vary greatly, many of your expenses won't. If you have a better than average month, plan ahead and recognize that at some point in the future you could run into a not so great month. Keep in mind that you may not know the exact dates your income will come in, and since you don't get to choose when your accidents or emergencies come up, you may very well have a need for extra money before your basic needs are handled.

Use the steps below to help with budgeting inconsistent income.

1. **DETERMINE YOUR AVERAGE MONTHLY INCOME.** The more months you can include, the better, but use at least three months to determine your average. If you've had a substantial windfall, or some other income that you know won't reoccur, don't include it. You need to create a *realistic* plan for your money. Utilizing any misleading information from the past will only hinder your planning.

2. **DECREASE NON-NECESSITIES.** Once you figure out your monthly average income, compare it with your monthly expenses. If your expenditures can only be met on your good months, then you have some cutting to do. Your expenses must be based on your average monthly income, *not* the great months that come few and far between. Anything that puts you over budget and can be labeled a "want," should be put aside until you can increase your income for at least three consecutive months.

Until you've increased your income for three consecutive months, delay spending on "wants" that put you over budget.

3. **CREATE A CUSHION.** To plan for unexpected events, I suggest a cushion in your budget of about 5 to 10%. Don't budget to the last penny. Every unexpected event doesn't have to be a state of emergency. What if you're away from home all day and really want to grab a burger? A couple of bucks shouldn't break the bank.

4. **DETERMINE A DOLLAR AMOUNT FOR YOUR OPPORTUNITY FUND.** No matter how inconsistent your income is, you must pay yourself before you pay anyone else if you ever expect to be wealthy. Some financial experts call this an "emergency fund," but I believe what

If you plan to become wealthy, you must pay yourself first.

you verbalize you magnify in your life. If you expect a rainy day, then you just might get a hurricane. Instead, create an "opportunity fund" to take care of any possibilities, good or not so good, that may come your way. This will also help you during the months when your earning is below average.

WILL MY CREDITORS REALLY MOVE MY DUE DATES TO FIT MY PERSONAL BUDGET?

Payment due dates can be inconvenient for a number of reasons. And while you might feel stuck, many companies will work with you. No one is out to cause you a financial hardship each month. These folks just want their money. And the more consistently you pay them on time, the better for all parties involved.

$ Real MONEY

If you need to, go online or call your creditor and request a due date change.

Contrary to popular belief, getting due dates changed is relatively easily. Different creditors have different policies on how, but most have a policy in place to get it done.

Here are a few steps to get due dates changed.

1. **SEEK HELP IMMEDIATELY.** Don't wait until you've missed a few payments or have been late excessively. On one hand, late payments show there's clearly a problem, but on the other, delinquency may weaken your negotiation power. Get help quickly, before you ruin your credit over something that has an easy fix.

2. **CHECK THE COMPANY'S WEBSITE FIRST.** Many credit card and utility companies plainly spell out what's required to change to a new due date. The information is usually found under a customer service related tab, and it will guide you through specific prompts to complete your request properly.

3. **CALL DIRECTLY.** If you can't find anything online or prefer to hold a live company representative accountable in case something goes wrong, then find the number to call on your statement or on the creditor's website. You'll almost certainly get an automated message, so listen

carefully to the available options and choose appropriately, or you'll waste a lot of time being transferred back and forth. When you get to a live person, specifically request to speak to someone who can assist you in changing your due date. Sometimes you'll be able to make the change over the phone, and other times you'll be told to go online or send the request in writing.

4. **WAIT FOR CONFIRMATION.** Unless you speak to a live person who confirms a new date and tells you when it will take effect, keep to your existing payment schedule. There will be a waiting period before you hear by mail or e-mail if you're approved for the change or not. Confirm the new due date on your next billing statement, and make on-time payments until then, and especially after.

SAVING AND REDUCING DEBT SIMULTANEOUSLY

TO MAKE REAL PROGRESS in your personal finances, drop the idea that you should handle savings and debt in an either/or fashion. No matter where I speak in the country, I'm always asked whether savings comes before or after paying down debt. And my response is always the same: it must be done simultaneously.

As I've said, you're either in the habit of creating wealthy habits or in the habit of not creating wealthy habits. Not saving *or* failing to pay down debt, at any stage in your personal finance journey, puts you in the category of not practicing a wealthy habit. Period. Even if you have to start off saving a relatively small amount while you pay down debt, to make the habit a part of your lifestyle, you have to start.

The beauty of getting organized and budgeting realistically is that you should now know exactly what you can put towards savings or debt. This isn't a question of whether you can afford to do both. You can't afford *not* to do both. If you need to shift your thinking, do so, and prepare to build savings and reduce debt simultaneously.

Real TALK
You can't afford not to save and pay down debt at the same time.

WHAT'S THE DIFFERENCE BETWEEN SHORT-TERM AND LONG-TERM SAVINGS?

Consistent saving helps you manage your money, plan for future needs, cope with unexpected expenses and emergencies, avoid borrowing and paying unnecessary interest, and ease financial stress. Still, understanding the difference between long and short-term savings helps you make more informed financial-planning decisions and ultimately make the best choices for you.

Long-term savings usually involve objectives like investing, retirement, and children's education. Short-term savings are what you typically hear referred to as your "emergency fund." (I prefer the term "opportunity fund.") This allows you to have money on hand to face life's financial hiccups, both planned and unplanned. Planned events include holidays like Christmas, that vaguely familiar time of year that seems to catch us all by surprise. Unplanned events include those moments when you find yourself on the side of the road with a flat tire or discover a busted water heater in your basement. When you don't have savings, these expenses typically end up on a credit card, making a bad situation much worse.

Real TALK

Without savings, unexpected expenses often end up on a credit card with a high interest rate, making a bad situation worse.

Beyond the "emergency fund," short-term savings may also include any large purchases you plan to make in the next one to five years, though funding these goals should come after your emergency money is saved. Major expenditures, like buying a home, planning a renovation or family vacation, expensive dental work, and anything your heart desires for the near future, requires short-term saving.

HOW MUCH DO I ACTUALLY NEED TO HAVE SAVED?

AFFIRM

I am clear about my goals and focused on intentionally bringing them forth.

The exact dollar amount you need to have saved can't be determined arbitrarily. While there are general rules of thumb, the reality is that your dollar amount will be determined by your particular circumstances and personal goals.

To figure out how much you need to save in a basic opportunity fund, review your budget and income, as well as fixed and variable expenses. You may have heard personal finance gurus say you should have six, nine, or twelve months of your monthly *expenses* socked away, but after going through a time when I had to lean on my savings, I beg to differ.

You should base your fund on multiple months of your *income*. This allows you to pad your expenses a bit, assuming your income exceeds your expenses, which it should. If you're out of work because of an accident, and you've only budgeted to pay your normal bills, how will you cover the increased medical debt, co-pays, and prescription costs that are sure to surface? If you lost your job, should you not be able to experience one moment of entertainment? Should you have to literally decide between eating and renting a movie from Redbox? You might still want to enjoy life and keep your energy up as you look to attract that next opportunity.

Real MONEY

Base the target amount of your opportunity fund on multiple months of income rather than monthly expenses.

Once you've gotten clear about what you actually want to save for, it's time to research costs and come up with an educated estimate. That amount will be added to your opportunity fund to determine how much cash you need to have saved in total.

In a plainly written formula, it looks like this:

OPPORTUNITY FUND + SHORT-TERM GOALS = TOTAL CASH RESERVE

SERIOUSLY! HOW CAN I POSSIBLY SAVE SIX MONTHS OF INCOME?

I don't know about you, but the first time someone nonchalantly told me to save enough money to cover six months of my expenses, I was instantly intimidated! I thought, "If I can't save $500 consistently, how in the world could I save several thousand?" If that was the key to this whole financial game, then, quite frankly, I felt locked out for life.

Real MONEY

Shift your focus from the larger goal. Saving is much easier when you do it in micro-steps.

Luckily, I learned early on that it doesn't have to be that hard. Instead of looking at a lofty goal that seemed so far out of reach, I decided to break my goal down into micro-steps. If you've been feeling your big saving goals are hopeless, here's what I suggest.

STEP 1: Determine what a great starting dollar amount would be for you. This isn't about what everyone else says or thinks, including the experts. I determined a goal that would seem like a big win for *me*! At the time, if I could get $500 in a savings account and not touch it for thirty days or more, I was totally winning!

STEP 2: Set your next milestone at $1000. Everyone can think of past personal obstacles that could've been easily overcome, if they'd only had $1000 in savings. *Savings make the difference between a crisis and an inconvenience.* Having $1000 tucked away can make the difference between getting that flat tire fixed on the spot and missing work and ticking off your boss again.

Savings make the difference between a crisis and an inconvenience.

STEP 3: Get one month of your net income stacked away. I've had people debate with me over whether this should be expenses or income. (See: *How much do I actually need to have saved?*) I don't know about you, but if some emergency comes up and I have to replace my income for a month, it would totally suck to come up short because I only planned for a specific set of expenses. Heaven forbid you'd like to pay your bills and still treat yourself to a bottle of water on a hot summer day.

STEP 4: Once you've achieved this huge step, pat yourself on the back, and increase your benchmark even further. Keep adding an additional month of net income to your savings goals until you get to at least six months of savings. The target date for each new goal is determined by the amount you can save each month. For example, if you can budget to save $125 each month, you'll have the first $500 in 4 months ($125 x 4 months = $500).

The example below is based on a monthly net income of $2200 with savings of $250 per month. It doesn't include any additional funds set aside for short-term savings.

I will have saved . . .	Amount	Target Date	Date Achieved
Starter Savings	$500	12/01/2014	12/29/2014
Minimum Savings	$1000	03/01/2015	02/20/2015
1 month of income	$2200	08/01/2015	
2 months of income	$4400	05/01/2016	
3 months of income	$6600	02/01/2017	
4 months of income	$8800	11/01/2017	
5 months of income	$11000	07/01/2018	
6 months of income	**$13200**	04/01/2019	

Doesn't this seem a little easier to accomplish than starting out to save $13,000? Imagine if you add in so-called windfalls, like tax refunds. You'll be there faster than you expect.

I'VE HEARD OF AN EMERGENCY FUND, BUT WHAT IS AN OPPORTUNITY FUND?

Several years ago, I wrote an article for the online magazine *Hello Beautiful* in which I called emergency funds dumb. Talk about backlash. Without even reading the article in its entirety, people left extremely mean comments, and the more zealous readers decided to email me personally and make sure I knew I was a dummy.

Real TALK

I don't use the term "emergency fund." I refuse to put words like "rainy day" and "emergency" next to my money.

Nevertheless, it hasn't stopped me from hitting the road and proclaiming at every church, college, and conference that lets me in the door that I don't believe in the term "emergency fund." Most of the money gurus in America have preached that having an emergency fund is the most basic and fundamental part of having a sound financial plan. Personal finance author and columnist Michelle Singletary suggests that you need at least three to six months of living expenses stashed away for a "rainy day." And frequent *Oprah* guest Suze Orman says, "Emergency cash is a necessity, not a luxury." While I love both of those money mavens and understand the logic behind their thinking, I totally disagree with putting alarming words like "rainy day" and "emergency" in such close proximity to my money.

What's appealing about saving for something bad? What's motivating about creating an account for when you lose your job or your car clunks out? What's stimulating about the thought of a major medical condition overtaking your loved one? It's no wonder more than 70% of America is living paycheck to paycheck. Some financial whiz thought scaring us into saving would work. Unfortunately, it seems to have scared us *away from* saving.

Associating money, something I consider positive, with an emergency, something I consider to be very negative in most instances, just doesn't make sense to me.

What you verbalize, you visualize and therefore run a greater chance of magnifying and magnetizing into your own life.

If you're running around worrying about saving your "emergency fund," what do you think will happen? You'll probably have an emergency! It's inevitable that your transmission will go out, your favorite cousin, who's been dating that loser for ten years, will finally decide to get married and have a destination wedding, and that running toilet you've been ignoring will create a $700 water bill—all in the same month.

So what's my answer?

THE OPPORTUNITY FUND:
AN ALTERNATIVE TO THE EMERGENCY FUND

We should save for opportunities, not for emergencies. Why not focus on the things in life you'd really like to magnify and bring forth? Why not save for a business venture, a dream vacation, a down payment on a home, or some other opportunity that would serve your soul? Why not save for a *sunny* day, the day you actually have the money to take care of something that both matters to you and enriches your life?

Will emergencies still arise? Of course. But now you have the opportunity to turn what would've been a crisis into a simple inconvenience.

There's nothing pleasant about an emergency, but knowing you can handle the situation with ease is definitely a blessing.

IF I SAVE ON MY OWN, DO I STILL NEED MY EMPLOYER'S RETIREMENT PLAN?

Your opportunity fund is essentially money you can access in case of an immediate need or opportunity. This is the money you tap into if your transmission goes out tomorrow or you experience unemployment for several months. It's not the money you bank on using to get you through your golden years. Your employer's retirement plan, on the other hand, is.

If your employer offers a retirement plan, thank your lucky stars. Many of your peers in the workforce wish they had that option. If your employer also offers a match to your contribution, you definitely want to be in position to contribute at least up to the match. It's free money, so don't leave it on the table.

Here's a look at some of the basic plans you may have access to, depending on your work place.

Real TALK

Any match your employer makes to your retirement plan contributions is free money. Don't leave it on the table.

401(K) PLAN: This is the plan you hear of most often. It's a corporate, pre-tax, contributory plan, which is payroll deducted and tax-deferred, with a selection of investment options. Most plans also include company matching with a vesting schedule based on years of employment.

403(B) PLAN: Very similar to the 401(k), this plan is a non-profit, pre-tax, contributory plan. It's usually extended to school teachers, church staff, and some other non-profit employees. It may be payroll deducted, and it grows tax-deferred. A variety of investment options are available. Some plans may provide company matching.

457 PLAN: This is a deferred compensation, pre-tax, contributory plan, which is payroll deducted and grows tax-deferred, with a selection of options. Most plans will provide minimal matching.

THRIFT SAVINGS PLAN: This government agency, pre-tax, contributory plan may be payroll deducted, and also grows tax-deferred with a selection of five managed investment options. This plan offers minimal agency matching.

SIMPLE IRA/401(K): Available through smaller companies, this pre-tax, contributory plan is payroll deducted and grows tax-deferred, with a selection of investment options. Normally there is a mandatory match, which boasts considerably lower administrative costs.

If you're self-employed, there are still investment retirement plans available to you.

SIMPLIFIED EMPLOYEE PENSION PLAN (SEPP): This plan allows a self-employed person to contribute pre-tax up to 15% of their net business profit, growing tax-deferred, with a self-directed selection of investment options.

YOU'RE INSANE! HOW COULD IT BE POSSIBLE TO SAVE TOO MUCH OR PAY DOWN TOO MUCH DEBT?

Well, I've been called way worse than insane, so that doesn't sting too much. Believe it or not, between my creation of the "opportunity fund" concept and telling people they're actually saving too much or paying down too much debt, I've been called crazy, and worse.

If you're on my mailing list, you know I frequently host complimentary educational calls on different personal finance and business topics. I'm proud of the fact that people all over the world who join the calls consider them to be high content and high value.

Yes, it is possible to save too much or pay down too much debt, if there's no room in your budget for those amounts.

Right before the recent tax deadline, I held a call entitled *5 Dumb Things Smart People Do with Tax Refunds*, and even though the line was muted, the tweets and Facebook posts afterwards confirmed what I thought might have happened. Women couldn't believe what they were hearing me say. That was the first time someone had broken down the truth about saving for them.

There are a few ways you can save too much. First, let's examine what happens when you come into a large sum of money, like a tax refund or an inheritance. If you save all the money, but have credit card debt, personal loans, or even a small student loan, then you're technically wasting money by continuing to pay high interest rates while earning little to no interest, depending on how and where you're saving the money.

More commonly, I meet with someone who decides to start saving without creating or consulting a budget. He arbitrarily chooses to authorize $100 per bi-weekly pay period to go to his savings account. Great start, right? Wrong! If all he can afford based on a realistic budget is $75 per month, he'll end up transferring that money right back out of the savings account to cover normal expenses. This isn't great for his savings, but it's even worse for his self-esteem. Initiating that transfer so quickly makes him feel like a failure at finances. He feels as if he can't save, and may even feel that something must be wrong with him. In reality, he *can* save, but he's saving too much for the particular stage he's in. He needs to adjust his expectations.

Paying off too much debt is almost the reverse of the saving example. If you use your refund to pay off debt or attempt to pay too much debt in one month without properly budgeting, but you don't have an opportunity fund in place, you're still not really making progress.

Let's say you use an entire tax refund to pay off a credit card balance in April, but in May you have an emergency. You have no savings, so what are you going to do? That's right. You're going to put that emergency expense on your credit card. By June, you end up right back in the scenario you were in before the refund came.

Instead, strategically pay down your debt. Definitely put a large chunk towards paying it down, if you can, but leave at least $1000 to the side in an account you can easily access when necessary.

WHAT ABOUT GOOD DEBT?

You've probably heard a bunch of bologna about accounts like mortgages and student loans being "good debt." But no debt is good. You may have to leverage debt in order to make progress in different instances, but that doesn't make it

Real TALK

Student loans and mortgages might help you get ahead, but that doesn't make them "good debt."

good. It's still just debt, and your objective should always be to have as little debt as possible. Falsely calling it "good," makes people too comfortable with thinking debt is okay somehow. In no instance is it okay. Keep your debt to a minimum, and always have a plan to pay it off. The best debts are the ones you don't owe anymore!

IS IT OKAY TO BUY STUFF WHILE I'M STILL IN DEBT?

Is this a trick question? No, it's not okay! The quickest way to get out of debt is to *stop* creating new debt. This is the time to sacrifice a little. Buying stuff is likely what got you into this predicament in the first place. You need to use every extra dime you can earn to relieve yourself of the debt you have now.

Real TALK

The quickest way to get out of debt is to stop creating new debt.

I'm not saying you can't treat yourself every once in a while, but for heaven's sake do *not* go around getting deeper in credit card debt or buying items that aren't an investment in your future. This is the time to get angry about the place you're in, so angry that your will to get out of debt supersedes any desire for more stuff.

If you must buy something, use cash. Credit cards are simply *not* an option. You and you alone, as misguided as you may have been by others, got yourself into this mess. This isn't the time to take the "I work hard, and I deserve it" stance. That sense of entitlement will keep you enslaved to debt forever.

WHAT IS A DEBT ELIMINATOR, AND HOW DO I DETERMINE MY DEBT-FREE DATE?

AFFIRM

I enjoy the flexibility financial freedom allows me.

I like to call the debt eliminator system the first cousin of the debt-snow-ball method, which you may be slightly more familiar with. I love using it in the *Mindset + Money Master Class*® because it gives each participant an opportunity to pinpoint the date they can be debt-free by simply implementing a few shifts in thought and behavior.

The debt-snowball method is a debt reduction strategy, whereby if you owe on more than one account, you pay off the accounts starting with the smallest balance first, while paying the minimum on all other debts. Once the smallest debt is paid off, you add that payment to what you're paying on the next one, working your way up the list, from smallest to largest. The process is continued until all debts are repaid.

The distinct difference in the debt eliminator system is that you use your budget to define the monthly dollar amount you'll allocate to pay down debt.

This isn't about using extra money to make debt payments. How often do most of us even have extra money? This is about reviewing your budget to uncover the amount you need for your debt pay-off plan. I want you to become intentional and strategic about the money you earn and make the conscious choice to shift from spending without a purpose to spending for the purpose of paying off your debt in half the time. This puts you in control and empowers you to make wise decisions for your money.

Here are the basic steps in the debt eliminator method.

STEP 1: **Complete your realistic budget.** You won't know the amount you can actually manage for your debt eliminator unless you budget first. If you start with fake numbers that you can't consistently pay, you'll just feel worse when you fall off after the first few months. The beauty of this system is setting a pay-off date and actively working towards it month by month.

STEP 2: **Determine your debt eliminator: the amount you'll apply to debt above monthly payments.** How much money in your current budget can be redirected towards the smallest debt?

STEP 3: **List all debts in ascending order, from smallest balance to largest.** You can also prioritize your debts in the order of the highest interest rate being charged, or by greatest amount owed. My recommendation is to pay off the smallest amount owed first, so you can achieve a win that much faster. The excitement and feeling of accomplishment will keep you on track with the remaining debts. If two debts are very close in amount owed, then the debt with the higher interest rate should be targeted for pay-off first. But again, it's your choice.

STEP 4: Pay the debt eliminator, the minimum payment plus the extra amount, towards that smallest debt until it is paid off. Note that some lenders, like mortgage lenders and car finance companies, will apply extra amounts towards the next payment. Contact your lenders in advance and tell them that the extra payments are to go directly toward principal reduction. They'll likely tell you to indicate your preference with each payment. Credit card companies don't typically need this instruction. The entire payment will go toward whatever the current balance is.

STEP 5: Commit to paying the minimum payment on every debt beyond the one you're actively working on. It won't do you any good to get behind on other payments.

STEP 6: Once an account is paid in full, apply your debt eliminator from that debt to the next account. Both the minimum payment and the extra amount should be added to the minimum payment of the next debt. This new sum becomes your new monthly payment for the second smallest debt.

STEP 7: Repeat until all debts are paid in full. Do each of these steps on paper first, using the amounts of your new monthly minimum payment to figure out when each debt will be paid in full. For simple numbers, divide the balance owed by the new minimum payment which has the debt eliminator built into it. This will tell you approximately how many months it should take to pay off that debt.

Keep in mind as you go along that you'll be paying the minimum on all other accounts, so adjust the balances of larger accounts by first subtracting however many months of minimum payments will go by, and then calculate how quickly you'll pay off the debt using the debt eliminator. If you do this all the way through, you'll find your approximate debt elimination date.

In the *Mindset + Money Master Class*®, I walk students through this process and provide them with a spreadsheet they can use to plug in their real numbers and determine when they can expect to be debt-free.

WHAT'S YOUR TAKE ON PAYDAY LOANS?

The Consumer Federation of America and the Federal Trade Commission have issued warnings to consumers about the dangers of predatory lenders and the possibility of innocent Americans becoming tangled in debt through the use of payday loans. Instant payday loans are easy to obtain, but getting rid of them isn't so easy.

UN REAL

When you factor in fees, payday loans often come with an APR of 250 to 650%.

The biggest problem with a payday loan is that a borrower often turns to one as a quick fix in dire financial circumstances. Because he's still in financial trouble when the loan comes due, he can't repay on time. A large percentage of payday loan customers extend the loans far beyond their next pay date. How can you expect to pay off the loan in full when your monthly bills continue to accrue? If you couldn't pay your bills last month, chances are you won't be able to pay those same bills, along with a new debt, this month. This reality usually doesn't hit people until it's too late, and the expensive payday loan debt has made a bad problem much worse.

Another problem with these loans is that they're generally extremely expensive. Lenders are supposed to provide an Annual Percentage Rate (APR) for every loan, but some payday loan companies use the term "finance fee" and do not reveal the true APR. For example, a fee of $20 per $100 for a payday loan may seem as if the lender is charging 20% interest, similar to many credit cards. However, the $20 fee per $100 is charged every two weeks. This fee is the equivalent of 26 times that credit card interest! Payday loans can have an APR of any- where from 250% to 650%.

HOW DO I KNOW IF I SHOULD JUST FILE BANKRUPTCY?

Real MONEY

The means test requires you earn less than the average income in your state, or meet other specific standards, to file Chapter 7.

Many people feel ashamed at the thought of having to file bankruptcy. They see it as a failure and an embarrassment, mostly because of the myths surrounding the process and its aftermath. The reality, however, is that not everyone finds themselves in these circumstances due to poor money management. Job loss, divorce, mounting medical bills, and a myriad of other personal setbacks can drive people into excessive debt and create unimaginable outcomes. When these things happen, bankruptcy may be the best option, but you have to understand those options and make the choice best for you.

In simple terms, bankruptcy is the legal process that allows individuals or businesses stuck in a financial crisis to settle their debts under a bankruptcy court's protection.

TWO MOST COMMON TYPES OF BANKRUPTCY:

CHAPTER 7 BANKRUPTCY - Chapter 7 bankruptcy is known as "straight bankruptcy" and is the preferred option for people with little or no property and a lot of unsecured debt. It's a liquidation bankruptcy, meaning the court will sell any non-exempt assets you have to pay your creditors and, regardless of the amount paid off, discharge that debt.

Since October 2005, there's been a means test applied to applicants for Chapter 7 Bankruptcy. You must earn less than the average income of

Bankruptcy filing won't discharge alimony, child support, student loans, or state and federal tax debts.

your state. (Check www.usdoj.gov/ust for means testing information). If you're above your state's median, then you can only file for Chapter 7 if your excess income cannot pay your debts over five years *and* cannot pay 25% of your unsecured debt over that period.

Chapter 7 bankruptcy doesn't discharge all debts. The filer is still responsible for student loans, as well as previous judgments on alimony and child support. State or federal tax bills must still be paid, and if you keep your home or car, all payments on these must be kept up.

CHAPTER 13 BANKRUPTCY - Chapter 13 bankruptcy, sometimes called the "wage earner's plan" or "reorganization bankruptcy," is quite different from Chapter 7 bankruptcy, which wipes out most of your debts. In a Chapter 13 bankruptcy, you use your income to pay some or all of what you owe to your creditors over time, anywhere from three to five years, depending on the size of your debts and income.

You must have a regular income and owe less than $250,000 in unsecured debt and less than $750,000 in secured debt. These debts must also be non-contingent and liquidated, meaning that they must be for a fixed amount and not subject to any conditions.

Always remember that despite the fresh start you hear about bankruptcy providing, there are definitely long-term implications. Chapter 7 bankruptcies remain on your credit history for ten years after the event, and Chapter 13 bankruptcies will stay on your history for seven years after you file. In addition, either filing will drop your FICO score a minimum of 100 points and an average of 250 points.

I'VE ALREADY FILED BANKRUPTCY. NOW WHAT?

If you've already filed bankruptcy and you're reading this book, you're on the right track. Besides doing obvious things like creating and sticking to a realistic budget, establishing an opportunity fund, and improving your overall mindset toward money, there are few steps you should consider.

1. **LET GO OF ANY GUILT OR SHAME.** At one time or another, we've all faced financial hardships. Between 2010 and 2011, over 3 million Americans filed personal bankruptcy, and over 6.5 million homes in the U.S. were foreclosed upon. Life happens to all of us. If this has been your experience, learn from it. Turn any pain around the subject into purpose. Dwelling on it, definitely won't make things better. Don't be fall for the myths and misconceptions about how horrible and incurable life after financial loss is. Ditch the embarrassment, get educated, and take the proper steps to bounce back.

Real TALK

Filing bankruptcy isn't the end of he world. Ditch the embarrassment, get educated, and take steps to bounce back.

2. **ENLIST THE HELP OF PROFESSIONALS.** Overcoming financial loss requires time and an intense dedication to financial discipline, but where can you turn for help? The National Foundation for Credit Counseling lists over seven hundred non-profit agencies nationwide at www.nfcc.org that can help you get back on your feet and set the strong foundation you need during this fragile time.

3. **CREATE SELF-IMPOSED CREDIT LIMITS.** If your bankruptcy included a substantial amount of unsecured debt, then you were likely maxed out on credit cards. In order to avoid ever being in that position again, and to demonstrate how responsible you are now with money, implement a self-imposed credit limit of 30% of whatever the banks may approve you for in the months following your discharge. If you're offered a $600 credit limit, for your purposes the card will never carry a balance of more than $200.

4. **APPLY FOR A SECURED CREDIT CARD.** If you're not instantly offered credit cards, or you're scared to use them, look into secured credit cards. You deposit a given amount of money, say $500, into a bank account and make it your credit limit. Charge small amounts, pay as agreed, and make sure the card reports to credit bureaus to ensure you're getting credit for this great behavior. Check out sites like www. creditcards.com and www.bankrate.com to identify the cards that work for you.

5. **PAY EVERY CREDIT REPORTING DEBT ON TIME.** After receiving this fresh start, it would be self-destructive to turn around and pay any open accounts late. It actually would come off as if you didn't quite learn your lesson, and while myth would have you believe it'll take ten years to reestablish your credit, you can do it much faster than that. Some filers are completely restored two years after discharge. If you've a missed a payment or made a late payment within those first twenty-four months, it'll be hard for creditors to trust you going forward.

Financial ruin, such as bankruptcy, is not the end of the world. You can choose to do something about it.

I'VE PRETTY MUCH PAID OFF ALL MY DEBT. NOW WHAT?

If you've banished credit card debt, student loans, car loans and the like, you're probably ready to start investing. Some people claim you can still invest while in debt, but if you can't afford to lose a little money without major repercussions, you probably should stay away from investing. People with little to no debt are usually more capable of weathering the storm you're likely to experience at different points on your investing journey.

When most people think about investing, they automatically think about buying stock. Stocks aren't bad, but they're not the only investment vehicle you have at your disposal, and investing everything in a single stock can be extremely dangerous. Below is a quick breakdown of a few practical vehicles that are available to you. Always consult a financial advisor to discuss your unique scenario.

STOCKS – Buying single stocks is extremely risky. When you put all of your money in one company, you're risking everything. That can be disastrous at any age!

BONDS – This is the next most commonly known investment vehicle. Bonds are basically a debt that a company owes, and you are the one loaning the company money. Bonds are just as risky as stocks, because if the company goes belly up, so does your entire investment.

ANNUITIES – An annuity is a contract between you and an insurance company that's designed to meet retirement and other long-range goals, under which you make a lump-sum payment or series of payments. In return, the insurer agrees to make periodic payments to you beginning immediately or at some future date. Annuities come in three forms: fixed, variable and indexed, so do your homework when finding the right fit.

MUTUAL FUNDS – A mutual fund is a vehicle through which groups of people will mutually invest in a fund that represents multiple companies. Your risk is lower, because unlike owning stocks or bonds in a single company, if one company in the fund goes down, but several others stay afloat, you won't go flat broke overnight.

REAL ESTATE – Since I was a real estate broker for over a decade, you're probably thinking I'll say real estate is a great investment vehicle. But real estate is only a great investment, when you can invest for the long term and do it without accruing ridiculous amounts of debt. I've been

Real MONEY

Only invest in real estate if you can do so for the long-term and without going deeply into debt.

fortunate enough to make some awesome investment decisions in this area. After college, I purchased a condo in Los Angeles from a probate estate for $160,000. Four years later, I sold it for nearly $300,000. Not bad, right? Well, in the meantime, I also bought a few rental properties in Charlotte and Dallas that were duds. They were duds not because anything was wrong with the houses, but because I was "too busy" to do my own due diligence. For every $1 I made on the condo I lived in, I *lost* $3 to $5 dollars on the other three properties. Moral of the story: Do your homework before you bank on real estate as your number one investment vehicle.

ISN'T BUYING A HOME A GREAT INVESTMENT AND SAVINGS TOOL?

Despite what you've heard, buying a home isn't for everyone. Unfortunately, many people who depended on their house as the ultimate savings tool quickly found out why a home is a place to rest your head, and not necessarily the best investment ever.

Before the Great Recession, many people who shouldn't have purchased homes in the first place bought a house because people said they should. They bought more house than they could afford, and many of them ended up worse off for it. Foreclosure rates skyrocketed, homeowners were forced into short sales, and many of those who held onto their homes found they were underwater on the mortgages.

The home-buying rules of the time told us:

1. to buy as much home as we could afford, or *qualify for*, with as little money down as possible.

2. to buy the biggest McMansion in the neighborhood, so everyone would know we made it.

3. we'd always make money, because homes always appreciate.

Now that we know how awful that advice was, it's time to figure out if you're ready to buy a home or not.

HERE ARE FIVE PERSONALITIES THAT MAY WANT TO WAIT BEFORE THEY BUY.

1. **THE WANDERER. Don't buy a home if you plan to live there for less than five years.** What's the point? 99.999% of your monthly mortgage payment will go towards interest and barely scratch the surface on your principal. Considering the amount of money it takes to make a down payment and then maintain the home, if you only plan on sticking around for a few years, then save yourself, your sanity, and your wallet the trouble and just rent until you think you're ready to settle in one place.

2. **THE NAIVE. Don't buy a home if you don't understand the market in your area.** Who cares what economists say about the national housing market? Understand the city in which you live. Every market is unique. Research the stability of the local job market with a specific focus on your potential industry or those you may be interested in over the long term. Check local foreclosure statistics. No matter how cheap your house was, if folks keep foreclosing at rapid rates, you may still lose money in the long run. Analyze how long homes in your area of interest stay on the market. If homes similar to those you're considering for purchase don't seem to resell well, you may consider changing your criteria.

3. **THE CHRONICALLY INDEBTED. Don't buy a home if more than 20% of your income is going towards DEBT, especially credit card debt.** Why make a bad thing worse? If you're having a difficult time paying off $5000, why would $200,000 be any easier? This also includes "good debt" like student loans. (Of course, the only good debt is the
If more than 20% of your income already goes to debt, don't buy a home. You're not ready yet.
debt you've paid off.) Contrary to popular belief, student loans *are* a factor, whether you're building a budget or examining debt ratios in

order to purchase a home. If anything, educational loans are the debt to be most concerned with, since not even bankruptcy can erase student loans.

Owning a home creates additional responsibilities and financial obligations. If a large portion of your income already goes towards debt, adding a mortgage won't improve your situation, so pay off as much as possible beforehand.

4. **THE ANTI-SAVER. Don't buy a home if you haven't saved for the down payment.** The days of 100% financing are basically over. You must have something to contribute in order to buy a home these days, ideally 10% to 20% down. The lender needs to know that you have a significant stake in this investment, and you won't just bail at the first sign of trouble. Putting some of your own hard earned money into the transaction demonstrates your commitment.

Saving for a down payment demonstrates your commitment to buying a home.

Although there are down payment assistance programs you should definitely go after, that should be an additional source of help, not the only source of a down payment. If you don't buckle down and strategically budget and manage your money before buying a home, trying to do so afterwards will be difficult. And remember, you may need money saved for more than just the down payment. Closing costs, all those fees associated with purchasing the home, are not always covered by the seller in the transaction.

5. **THE UNREALISTIC. Don't buy a home if you don't have a reserve account for repairs and regular maintenance.** The week after your deal closes, a toilet will overflow or a pipe will burst. Things beyond your control will inevitably happen, and you must be prepared tackle them head on. There's no taking the repair cost out of your mortgage like you may have taken it out of your rent. With home ownership, those days are so gone! And beware, because home warranties and homeowners insurance don't cover everything. Stash away at least $1000 above what you save for your down payment, closing costs, and of course, furniture, so that when you do move in, a household inconvenience doesn't become a life catastrophe.

Owning a home isn't for everyone at every time. I'm not saying you'll never buy a house, but make sure when you do, you're actually ready for all that comes with it. Qualifying for a mortgage doesn't mean you can afford everything it takes to maintain a home.

BOOSTING CREDIT

KINDA HARD TO REALLY work on something and get results when you don't know much about it. All most adults know is that they want "good credit," because bad credit sucks, is extremely expensive, and seriously limits your options in everything from where you can live, to what you can buy, and where you can work these days. Sound about right?

You may literally be starting from scratch and need to build credit. You may have credit that you haven't checked in years because you're afraid of how low the score might be. Or you may have stellar credit and get more offers for credit lines than you know what to do with. No matter where you are on your money journey, it pays to know how to improve your credit.

If you haven't completed Sections 1 and 2 of this book, I should warn you that this chapter won't mean a hill of beans to you. Nothing I say in the next few pages will have any major impact on you, your credit. How do I know? Because people always come to me wanting to "fix their credit." Your credit is only a result. It's a consequence of certain actions that originated in specific thoughts and beliefs you've had about different circumstances—those circumstances you created and those you may have fallen into for reasons beyond your control. You can get all the information and education in the world, but if your mindset doesn't change, knowing the ABC's of credit won't change a thing either.

Real
TALK

Your credit status, good or bad, is a consequence of your actions, which originated in your thoughts and beliefs.

Well, you've been warned, so without further ado, let's talk about boosting credit.

HOW DO I OBTAIN A COPY OF MY CREDIT REPORT?

To keep your credit clean, you have to know what's reflected on it. If you've been avoiding it, it's time to face this thing once and for all. Get in the habit of checking your credit report no less than once a year. Even though you know you pay your bills on time, checking your credit report consistently will alert you of inaccuracies on your credit file or signs of potential identity theft.

Request a free copy of your credit report by visiting www.annualcreditreport.com or contacting the Annual Credit Report line at 877-322-8228. Be aware that you'll likely be asked to pay a fee in order to view the full report with the score. The free report is sufficient, if you believe your credit is in good standing, but if you've had any credit challenges or are planning a big purchase in the near future, it's important that you choose the version with the score. See where you stand and develop quantifiable goals.

You may also obtain your credit report by contacting any of the three major credit agencies directly.

Experian	Equifax	TransUnion
PO Box 949	PO Box 740241	PO Box 1000
Allen, TX 75013	Atlanta, GA 30374	Chester, PA 19022
888-397-3742	800-685-1111	800-888-4213
www.experian.com	www.equifax.com	www.transunion.com

WHAT INFORMATION SHOULD I EXPECT TO SEE ON MY CREDIT REPORT?

Credit reports are sometimes very hard for the untrained eye to review. Study yours until you spot and can fully understand these five main categories of information.

1. **PERSONAL INFORMATION:** Verify your name, current and previous addresses, social security number, telephone number, date of birth, and current and previous employers.

2. **CREDIT HISTORY:** The majority of your credit report is comprised of information on credit accounts that have been opened in your name. Details about these accounts include the date the account was opened, the credit limit or amount of the loan, the payment terms, the balance, and a history of your payment records on each account. Closed or inactive accounts, depending on the manner in which they were paid, stay on your report for seven to eleven years from the date of their last activity.

3. **CREDIT SCORE:** This three digit number is issued by each of the major credit bureaus and is used to help potential creditors decide how likely it is they'll be repaid in a timely manner. (See: *What's a credit score, and how is it determined?*)

4. **CREDIT INQUIRIES:** Each time a third party, such as a creditor, potential lender, or insurer pulls your credit report, it's recorded on your file as a credit inquiry. Inquiries may remain on your credit report for up to two years.

5. **PUBLIC RECORDS:** Public records obtained from government sources, including bankruptcies, tax liens, collections, judgments, and records of overdue child support are also recorded on your credit report. Public information stays on your credit report for up to seven years.

WHAT SHOULD I DO IF THERE ARE ITEMS ON MY CREDIT REPORT I DON'T RECOGNIZE?

It's extremely important to look over your credit report with a fine-tooth comb as soon as possible. If you discover any mistakes, immediately contact all three credit bureaus by either disputing online or by certified mail. No matter how large or small the discrepancy, you need to alert them of the mistake and request that they investigate the matter and subsequently change or remove the item as needed. If you don't get an email or reply in writing within thirty to sixty days, don't just drop it. Send another letter reminding the credit agencies that they are required by law to investigate any incorrect information or provide an updated credit report with the incorrect information corrected or removed.

A sample Dispute Letter is included in Appendix B in order to assist you in drafting your own.

WHAT'S A CREDIT SCORE, AND HOW IS IT DETERMINED?

A credit score, often referred to as a FICO score, is a three-digit number potential creditors use to help them decide how likely it is they'll get paid back on time. It's also called a risk score because it helps lenders predict the risk that you won't be able to repay the debt as agreed.

Scores are generated by using elements from your credit report, as well as other sources, such as your credit application, at the time a lender requests your credit report. Credit scores are fluid numbers that change as the elements in your credit report change. For example, payment updates or a new account may cause scores to fluctuate within a few days.

The designers of credit scoring models review a set of consumers, often over a million individuals. The credit profiles of these consumers are examined to identify common variables. The designers then build statistical models that assign weights to each variable, and these variables are combined to create a credit score. Model builders strive to identify the set of variables from a consumer's past credit history that most effectively predicts future credit behavior.

Your credit rating is calculated by compiling information in the following five categories.

1. Payment history constitutes 35% of the rating. A pattern of late payments will cause a huge drop in your credit rating, especially if you see your score within weeks of the late payment.

2. The duration of your credit history accounts for 15% of your rating. The longer you maintain positive lines of credit, the better. This is why even if I advise clients to stop accruing new credit, I rarely advise them to call the creditor and close the line down completely.

3. New credit counts for 10%, so don't make a habit of applying for credit unnecessarily. This is especially true if you already have outstanding credit accounts carrying significant balances. To potential creditors, it appears as if you've made a lifestyle out of living off credit.

4. The mix of credit used is 10% of your rating. This measures how much of your debt is installment debt versus revolving debt. (See: *What's the difference between installment debt and revolving debt?*)

5. The current amount of total debt counts for 30% of your overall credit rating.

WHAT'S THE DIFFERENCE BETWEEN INSTALLMENT DEBT AND REVOLVING DEBT?

INSTALLMENT DEBT

Installment debts allow you to pay a fixed portion of the total amount borrowed at regular intervals over the life of the loan. The use of installment debt often allows you to purchase items at a competitive interest rate. The loan is paid back using an amortizing schedule or monthly payments of a fixed amount over the entire life of the loan. At first, most of the monthly payment goes to pay your interest. The latter installments go to paying down your principal. The fixed payment amount allows you to easily budget for the monthly payment. It also allows you to have a payoff date in sight.

Real **TALK**

Using credit cards to buy things you can't afford is the easiest way to financial ruin.

REVOLVING CREDIT

A revolving line of credit, also called open-ended credit, is made available for your use at any time. Revolving credit usually comes in the form of major credit cards, such as Visa or MasterCard, as well as department store cards. At the time of application, your previous payment history, as well as income, will usually determine your credit limit. Once you use the credit card, you're required to make monthly minimum payments based on the total balance outstanding that month.

Despite how easy it is to obtain this type of credit, or how convenient it may be, this is the easiest way to financial ruin, if you don't use discretion with your credit card purchases. The average interest rate on such cards can be 18% or more, plus annual fees. Impulsive buying, failure to compare the cost of buying with cash versus using a credit card, and purchasing unnecessary items that you simply cannot afford are all part of the demise brought on in pursuit of "convenience."

It can be nearly impossible to pay off credit cards by paying the minimum monthly payment.

A concern with revolving credit is that it's more difficult to prepare for your future monthly payment, as rates and terms may fluctuate based on the very, very fine print in your agreement. It can be nearly impossible to pay off your debt by paying the minimum payment required by creditors, and they know this. Creditors are not lending you money for charity. This is a business, and their sole intent is to make as much money as possible. As you pay down your debt, the minimum payment is also reduced. This does nothing but extend your pay-off period and, consequently, the interest you pay.

CAN I BUILD OR REBUILD CREDIT WITHOUT CREDIT CARDS?

There are several ways you can build credit if you wish to stay clear of credit cards altogether, but keep in mind that the best credit scores are earned by successfully utilizing a mix of different credit types, including revolving and installment accounts.(See: *What's the difference between installment debt and revolving debt?*)

Below are a few tips for building credit without conventional credit cards. Remember that the only way to build credit is to ensure that, no matter what method you choose, the credit line is being reported to the three major credit bureaus. If not, you won't be building credit. You'll just be wasting time and possibly money.

1. **GET AN INSTALLMENT LOAN.** Applying for a small installment loan from your local credit union or bank may be an ideal way to begin your credit profile. Keep the length of the loan short, no more than twenty-four months, and make sure you're using the money to purchase something worthwhile. Good choices include something that will benefit your business or career, such as a laptop or other necessity. This should help you build credit, while limiting the amount of interest you pay, and you'll be able to consistently budget for the small monthly payment.

2. **APPLY FOR A SECURED CREDIT CARD.** Used properly, credit cards can be useful financial tools. Applying for a secured version of a credit card simply means you make a deposit to the issuing bank or credit union, and you get a card with a credit limit of that amount, similar to a pre-paid card. Be careful with this method because there can be outrageous application and annual fees, which eat away at the money you deposit. If you bank with one, your credit union would be a good place to look for a secured card. Try to obtain a card that has no application fee and a very low annual fee. Choose one that converts to a regular, unsecured credit card after twelve to eighteen months of on-time payments.

Be careful with secured cards. Some carry high application and annual fees, which eat away at your deposit.

3. **BECOME AN AUTHORIZED USER.** If someone you trust is getting a loan, you can ask to co-sign with them so that your credit will be linked with theirs. But only do this if you're *confident* the person will pay the loan off diligently. Any irresponsibility on their part will negatively affect your credit score for the life of the loan. (See: *How can co-signing on a loan for someone else affect me?*)

4. **BUILD YOUR OWN PAYMENT HISTORY.** Payment Reporting Builds Credit is an alternative credit bureau that gathers data on rent and recurring payments for cable, cell phone, insurance, utility, and other bills. This may be beneficial when applying for some limited forms of credit, but it's not recognized by all lending institutions.

HOW DO I BEGIN TO CLEAN UP MY CREDIT NOW?

Real TALK

You have to decide you deserve a life of abundance, not a life of bondage to material possessions.

1. **MAKE UP YOUR MIND.** In order to clean up your credit and avoid falling into the same trap again, you have to make up your mind now that you deserve to live a life of abundance, not one in bondage to material possessions. Decide today that if the normal American lives paycheck to paycheck, you're 100% comfortable with being abnormal.

2. **STOP USING CREDIT CARDS.** When you use cash, you'll think a lot harder about whether your purchase is really a necessity. Cut up any department store credit cards and put a major credit card in a safe place for an emergency or opportunity. Do *not* call the credit card companies and close the accounts. That will erase the history as soon as the creditor sends the next update to the credit bureaus, usually within thirty days, and you'll see your score drop.

3. **WRITE DOWN ALL OF YOUR DEBT.** List each debt you're responsible for along with its current balance owed, interest rate, and minimum monthly payment. (See: *What is a debt eliminator, and how do I determine my debt-free date?*)

4. **KNOW YOUR DUE DATE.** Late payment fees can cost you an average of $40 per month. This is a complete waste of money. Always pay on time or early.

5. **NEGOTIATE LOWER INTEREST RATES.** Call your creditors and convince them to lower the interest rate by at least 25%. If you've made most payments on time and don't have any negative payment history, many credit card companies will work with you. They'd rather do that than take the chance that you'll default and not pay them at all. (See: *What should I say once I get my creditor on the phone?*)

6. **BALANCE TRANSFER WHEN APPROPRIATE.** Transfer high interest credit cards to other cards which may be offering 0% interest for a specified period of time, but be careful to not make this strategy a way of life. The point is

to help you get out of debt by utilizing the least amount of money you possibly can.

7. **PAY MORE THAN THE MINIMUM.** Credit card minimum payments are calculated to make it easy for you to carry the debt for as long as possible. When you pay more than the minimum, you cut down on the interest and pay the principal down more quickly. (See: *What is a debt eliminator, and how do I determine my debt-free date?*)

HOW DO I KEEP THE CREDIT CARDS I HAVE IN GOOD STANDING?

If you've already begun to cultivate a positive relationship with credit cards, recognizing them as a financial tool and not a crutch, then use the following tips to keep up the good work.

1. **DON'T CHARGE MORE THAN 30% OF THE CARD'S LIMIT.** If your credit limit is $1,000, never carry a balance of more than $300 for longer than thirty days.

2. **DON'T JUGGLE MORE THAN TWO MAJOR CREDIT CARDS AT THIS POINT.** The easiest way to turn this into a negative situation is to overextend your use of credit. With all of your financial objectives to consider, don't complicating things.

3. **DON'T CHARGE MORE THAN YOU CAN PAY OFF IN A MONTH.** Accruing unnecessary interest is not what builds credit. Using the card responsibly does.

4. **IF AN EMERGENCY ARISES, USE A PORTION OF THE CASH YOU'VE SAVED FIRST AND PUT THE REMAINDER ON CREDIT, IF NECESSARY.** I can guarantee you that the interest you'll pay on the credit card is more than you're earning on your savings account.

5. **PAY YOUR BILLS ON TIME.** If you can, set your credit cards up on an automatic bill pay system to be paid on or before the due date. This way, you'll avoid the risk of any additional fees accruing because you missed the due date by even one day. Make sure the date you choose is one when

you know the money is guaranteed to be in your account. You don't want to incur a hefty overdraft fee from your bank either.

6. **USE YOUR CARDS REGULARLY TO ENSURE THAT YOUR REPORT IS UPDATED REGULARLY.** This will also keep the lender interested in you as a customer. If you get a credit card and never use it, the issuer could cancel the account. For credit scores to be generated, you have to have had credit for at least six months, with at least one of your accounts updated (or used) in the past six months.

7. **PROTECT YOURSELF FROM CREDIT CARD FRAUD.** Don't ever give your credit card number to someone over the phone or over the Internet, unless you're positive you're dealing with a reputable company or trusted site.

8. **IF YOU BELIEVE YOUR CARD HAS BEEN LOST OR STOLEN, REPORT IT IMMEDIATELY.** You won't be held responsible for charges incurred if it's reported before someone else uses it. The longer you wait, the more likely you are to have difficulties with the process. Policies vary from company to company. If you think your card is lost somewhere you'll eventually find it, have it temporarily suspended.

SHOULD I CLOSE A CREDIT CARD ONCE I PAY IT OFF?

Paying off a credit card is definitely something to celebrate. But closing the account might be the fastest way to cut the party short. If you've been working long and hard on your debt, you don't want to get to the end of the road and blow it now.

Closing a paid-off credit card can damage your credit score. Closing a delinquent account with a balance due will damage it even more.

It may seem logical that paying a credit card off and closing it will make your credit score shoot up, but closing a credit card account, even one you've paid off, can actually hurt your score. And if you've heard over the years that closing a credit card that's delinquent will help or magically make it go away, you've heard wrong. Not only is that not the case, closing a delinquent card with an outstanding balance due will further damage your credit.

There are only a few instances when closing your credit card might make good sense. One is when you've experienced identity theft. Closing the account might be the only way to stop the fraudulent behavior, and more than likely your creditor will advise that the account be closed. Another reason would be if it's a relatively new credit card that you don't plan to use. If you already have other open cards, and this one doesn't have a balance, then no harm, no foul. If you have a card that for some reason springs new terms on you, like an increased interest rate or annual fee, then you have to do what you have to do. In actuality, the credit card issuer would probably close the credit card for you if you decided to reject the new terms. Try to negotiate the new terms or let the company know you're considering closing the account, before actually doing it.

Here are a few instances when you *shouldn't* close a credit card account.

1. **DON'T CLOSE YOUR OLDEST CREDIT CARD ACCOUNT.** Your credit history makes up 15% of your total credit score. Closing out your old credit cards shortens your overall credit history. The longer your history, the better. It gives potential creditors a clear picture of your long-term habits. Lenders tend to view borrowers with short credit histories as riskier. While closing the oldest credit card may not impact your credit score immediately, years down the road you could experience a sudden and unexpected credit score drop once it's time for that closed account to fall off the report.

2. **DON'T CLOSE ANY CREDIT CARD THAT STILL HAS A BALANCE.** When you close a credit card with a balance, your total available credit and credit limit are reported as $0. If you still have a balance on the card with no credit limit, it looks like you're maxed out. A maxed out credit card, or one that *appears* to be maxed out, will have a highly negative impact on your credit score. Remember that your level of credit card debt, including your credit to debt ratio, is 30% of your credit score.

3. **DON'T CLOSE THE ONLY CREDIT CARD THAT ACTUALLY HAS AVAILABLE CREDIT.** Again, 30% of your credit score assesses how much available credit you possess versus your total credit limit. Closing out this card will decrease total available credit and, therefore, increase your total credit utilization.

Basically, whereas it appeared you were managing your credit card well and not maxed out or dependent on it, when you close it, your score is based more on the other accounts you still have. If those still have balances, then you may appear maxed out on all your open accounts.

4. **DON'T CLOSE THE ONLY CREDIT CARD YOU HAVE.** Since 10% of your credit score is based on the different types of credit you have, keeping a credit card in the mix will add points to your score. Leave your only credit card open to show that you have experience with this type of account. After all, most of the other accounts you'll have are likely installment loans, which are somewhat easier to manage, since the monthly payment stays the same. Dealing with the fluctuations of credit card payments demonstrates a different money-management skill.

WHAT SHOULD I SAY ONCE I GET MY CREDITOR ON THE PHONE?

Did you know that the voices on the other end of the phone when you call a creditor belong to normal people like you and me? For the most part,

Real TALK

Your attitude will determine how successful you are when you negotiate with your creditors by phone.

these are awesome people just trying to make a living like the rest of us. They're human, and they've experienced real life, including the ups and downs of the economy, and other triumphs and failures, just like you. So don't let the horror stories you've heard about shady characters, or even your own past experiences, keep you in fear.

Your attitude toward the customer service representatives and toward the process has to be in order before you pick up the phone. Your attitude will determine your success with the process. Don't call when you're fearful or angry. It won't do you any good, nor will it achieve your desired result. The Golden Rule will truly serve you in speaking to your creditors. Treat them how you'd want to be treated. It'll go a long way in a world where many people who contact them call with chips on their shoulders.

When you call, have a goal in mind. Be deliberate. Don't call "just to see," or you'll get suckered into results you don't want and probably end up with a bunch of other crap you don't need. The fact that you're the one calling means you control the conversation. So set the stage from the onset by announcing, "I'm calling to discuss . . . ."

If you're looking to settle a debt or enter into some type of repayment, use phrases like "My budget is" and "I can comfortably afford." Remember everything comes back to the budget. It's the key to your savings plan and to your debt elimination plan. Don't get talked into something you can't afford and make a bad situation worse. Trust me. The creditor prefers to get you in an agreement you can keep over the long run.

No matter how polite and prepared you are, you may get an idiot on the other line. If you do, remember you called, so you're in control. Tell that person something just came up and you'll call back later. Don't stop trying like many people do. One person's bad attitude shouldn't keep you from achieving your goals.

WHAT SHOULD I DO IF I'M BEING HARASSED BY A CREDITOR?

If you're being harassed, I'm going to assume you've fallen behind on your obligations. If that's the case, make sure you plan to eliminate that debt. (See: *How Do I Begin to Clean Up My Credit Now?*)

Now that we have that out of the way, please know you're not the first to fall behind on your credit card payments, and you certainly won't be the last. One of the reasons banks are willing to take a risk and issue cards to people who may not be able to pay on time, is that they make a fortune on the fees associated with the negligence and naïveté of some borrowers. Nevertheless, you do have rights, and you should not be harassed.

According to the Federal Trade Commission's published interpretation of the Fair Debt Collection Practices Act, collectors cannot continuously call you. Section 806(5) prohibits contacting the consumer by telephone "repeatedly or continuously with intent to annoy, abuse, or harass any person at the called number." "Continuously" means making a series of telephone calls, one right after the other. "Repeatedly" means calling with excessive frequency under the circumstances.

If you feel you are being harassed according to the guidelines above, you should try the following.

1. **DO NOT IGNORE THE CREDITOR, ESPECIALLY WHEN YOU KNOW YOU'RE IN THE WRONG.**
    Acknowledge the breakdown in communication and explain any financial hardship. Make an attempt to resolve the situation. With the number of individuals defaulting on credit cards, smart collectors will be happy to help you create a repayment plan that fits your budget.

2. **KEEP A JOURNAL OF THE DAYS AND TIMES OF CALLS, AS WELL AS THE METHODS OF CONTACT.** You'll need this in order to establish that the creditor's efforts are indeed "continuous" and "repeated."

3. **NOTIFY THE CREDITOR BY PHONE IF YOU FIND THAT THEIR CONTACT IS ACTUALLY ABUSIVE.**
    Advise them that you know your rights, that you don't wish to be harassed in such a manner, and that you'd prefer your communication by mail. Verify your mailing address with them, and make an arrangement to handle your debt, if you haven't yet done so.

4. **IF THE HARASSMENT CONTINUES, NOTIFY THE CREDITOR BY CERTIFIED MAIL.** A sample letter is included in Appendix B at the back of this book to assist you in drafting your own.

HOW DO I PREVENT IDENTITY THEFT?

Identity thefts result in fraud amounts of up to $54 billion per year.

Don't be fooled. Just because you haven't been fully exposed to the reality of identity theft, doesn't mean you're exempt. Researchers say that if you haven't experienced identity theft already, you know someone who has. According to the Federal Trade Commission, stolen identity was the number one complaint from 1999 to 2010, and fraud amounts averaged between $48 and $54 billion per year. With our growing dependency on social media and cellphones, we're more exposed to potential identity theft than ever before.

In this day and age, what can you do? Many of us use these technological means to stay connected to the world and expand our businesses, so hiding from them isn't going to do the trick, no matter how many privacy settings you have on Facebook.

Here are a few things you can do to protect yourself from this costly epidemic.

1. **LOOK AT HOW YOU RECEIVE YOUR MAIL AND IMPORTANT DOCUMENTS.** In many neighborhoods, you're at the mercy of trusting every person who walks by your mailbox. We like to hope everyone will be honest, but it doesn't always work that way. Switch to online or paperless statements from your financial institutions and other service providers, or think about utilizing a P.O. Box. Both require a little more work, but not nearly as much as dealing with the headache of a stolen identity.

2. **MONITOR YOUR FINANCES ROUTINELY.** Far too often, people don't realize their finances have been compromised until it's pretty late in the game and too much damage has been done. For many people getting the mail out of the mailbox is one thing, but actually opening it up and reading it is another. You need to know what's going on with anything associated with your name and social security number. Don't ignore envelopes from companies you didn't open an account with. If they're sending you correspondence, someone else may have opened an account in your name.

3. **CHECK YOUR CREDIT OFTEN.** By "often," I mean more than that one time of year you can get the free report from annualcreditreport.com. You can find credit monitoring services through your financial institution or the credit bureaus. You want to receive an alert as soon as a new account is applied for or opened in your name.

4. **USE MORE THAN ONE PASSWORD.** I know, I know. It seems like too much trouble to memorize all these passwords, but if it keeps a crook off your heels and out of your wallet, isn't it worth it? Use PINs and passwords with numbers, symbols, and upper and lowercase letters that are difficult to guess. If I know your spouse's name and children's names ten minutes after meeting you and can use that information to crack your passcodes, you probably need to put a little more creativity into it.

5. **TRY OUT AN IDENTITY PROTECTION SERVICE.** Think about this like car insurance. You can have a black belt in defensive driving, but the reality is you're

still at the mercy of other drivers. If someone hits you, isn't it great to be able to call your insurance company and have them handle all of the paperwork, phone calls, and negotiations? If your identity is stolen, identity protection services can do the exact same thing.

Did you know that the average victim spends 165 hours working to close accounts opened in his or her name due to ID theft? They spend another fifty-eight hours correcting problems on existing accounts. Unless you can take three full weeks off of work to make this your full-time job, you may want to consider identity protection. Look specifically for services like Protect My ID, offered by the credit bureau Experian. Not only do they assign a person to handle your case and cut down the time you'd otherwise spend getting your life back together, they offer credit monitoring to ensure it'll never happen again.

Every day, somewhere in this country, an identity theft victim loses the opportunity to realize his or her dreams. Whether it's the opportunity to obtain financing for a mortgage or an auto loan, or to take out a student loan to complete a degree, dreams are crushed because of lack of planning and preparation in this area. Get serious about making sure it doesn't happen to you.

RELATIONSHIPS AND MONEY

"The strength of the team is each individual member. The strength of each member is the team." - Phil Jackson

MONEY IS A CONSTANT factor in your relationships. You inherited financial blueprints from people who influenced you in your youth. Money is intertwined in your romantic relationships from the first date, and if you have children, you're one of their greatest money influences. No matter how well you create wealthy habits, how much more money you earn, or how wisely you manage your money, you can still find yourself making financial fumbles if you don't learn to manage the connection between your money and your loved ones.

If you're married or in a committed relationship, the two of you have to work as a team, agree on financial goals, and take on roles that allow you to play to your strengths. You should both be informed of all the important details and involved in decision-making, but that doesn't mean you each take on the same responsibility. If one of you is better at creating a budget and the other is better at reconciling the accounts, you should each handle what you do best. Linebacker Ray Lewis made thirty-one interceptions over the seventeen seasons he played for the Baltimore Ravens, but he didn't stop halfway through and try to step into the quarterback's role. The only way a football team functions well is for every player to play his or her assigned position. The same applies to the team that consists of you, your wife or girlfriend, and your children.

Even when you're not in a serious romantic relationship or don't have children, you still have to be aware of how your friends and family members affect your bottom line and how money affects those relationships. According to a money etiquette survey from 2007, 57% of people surveyed acknowledged that they'd seen familial relationships or friendships ruined by a failure to pay back money loaned. It can get ugly. Children sue their parents, neighbors and best friends battle over broken promises, and brothers and sisters take sibling rivalry to a whole new level. And money's at the center of it all.

UN REAL

A survey found that 57% of people have seen a relationship ruined due to one party's failure to repay the other.

You must learn to communicate effectively about the subject of money. You can't have a great relationship with anyone on any level until you learn how to have money discussions from how to split the check after dinner to whether or not you can help someone make their rent. It's not always easy, but if you don't learn to manage conflicts and have civilized conversations about money, you risk losing the relationships you enjoy with friends and relatives. You can be reactive or proactive, but the topic of money will come up in your relationships over and over again. How you handle it is up to you.

YOUR HONEY, YOUR MONEY

O N A 2012 LIST of Top 10 reasons couples divorce, money finally slipped down to number four. But guess what rose to the top. Communication breakdown. For many people, the issue happens to be communicating about money.

Where does all this poor communication start? Think about your dating relationships, past or present. Money is the one subject folks will lie about most when they're testing the dating waters with someone new. People tend to stretch the truth a bit when it comes down to talking about the dollar. They do all kinds of things to influence how others perceive their finances.

While some conceal their money to be certain they're not being exploited for it, others spend money they don't have in an attempt to impress the objects of their affection. Some people hide behind a facade of the disciplined fiscal manager to cover up the fact that their finances are in complete shambles. This may work in surface level interaction, gentlemen, but when dating becomes a full-blown relationship, it's time to get real.

When disagreements arise around "little" financial issues, they often lead to much bigger challenges. From shared financial responsibilities to unequal earning, we don't want these issues to snowball into the other top causes of divorce: infidelity and physical, psychological, or emotional abuse. It's time to talk money with your honey!

WHAT ARE THE WARNING SIGNS OF A
FINANCIALLY IRRESPONSIBLE PERSON?

Before dating becomes "I do," look for warning signs of risky financial behavior. If you find them, act accordingly.

She looks put together, drives a new BMW, and lives in a nice neighborhood. She steps out every day in designer clothes and shoes with a designer bag hanging from her arm. On the surface, a lot of women look like they have it all together.

But just like no one can look at you and see your financial history, you can't determine a woman's financial savvy by looking at her. No matter how financially successful a person looks on the outside, it's up to you to be alert and pay attention to the waving red flags that make it clear the woman who caught your eye may be a mess when it comes to money.

People who end a marriage over bad money habits didn't develop those habits after they married. They had them all along, and the signs were there. Before dating becomes "I do," look for these warning signs and clues. If you find them, run or sign up for some serious premarital counseling before walking down the aisle.

RED FLAG #1: She drives a late model Mercedes and always looks like she stepped out of the pages of a magazine, but she lives with roommates or her parents for no clear reason.

RED FLAG #2. She's constantly asking you to lend her money or help her pay a bill.

RED FLAG #3: She leaves her mail in the mailbox for days at a time, and when she brings it in, the envelopes are stamped "Past Due" or "Urgent."

RED FLAG #4: She never answers her phone when you're around, and the calls she ignores are from 800 numbers.

RED FLAG #5: She doesn't have a bank account and says she prefers to use a prepaid debit card because it's "easier."

If you have your finances on the right track, or you're making strides to get them there, you must be careful of the company you keep, especially those you choose to date. Although you may have the best of intentions to help her get her finances straight, it's much easier for her to screw yours up. Don't ignore the signs. They're all around you, if you just pay attention.

ARE THERE QUESTIONS I SHOULD ASK ABOUT MONEY WHILE WE'RE DATING?

While you're definitely on point in your desire to have an upfront money conversation with the woman in your life, don't get the questions completely out of order. When we first start dating someone, we all too often jump straight into asking how much money they make. If we like what we hear, we stick around. But there are bigger issues, like financial compatibility and responsibility.

Real TALK

"How much do you make?" is definitely not the first money question you should ask when you're dating.

Here are a few appropriate questions to get your financial discussions rolling.

1. *How did your parents handle money?*
We all have a financial blueprint, the way we specifically interact with our money. For most of us, this was handed down to us by our parents, almost like a strand of DNA. But it's important to remember no one is born with a particular attitude towards money. We were all taught specific ways to think about and deal with money matters. These conscious and subconscious beliefs, ideals, thoughts, and actions are what create our financial blueprint.

Talk to each other about what you've heard about money and what types of behaviors you've witnessed regarding money and financial matters. Once you understand the environment a person grew up in, or the way her parents or other influential people in her life handled money, it'll be much easier and much less frustrating to understand her money style.

2. *What does money really mean to you?*

When it comes to our relationships, money is *not* the issue many people believe it is. Money, that little green piece of paper in your wallet, in and of itself, is powerless. It's actually what the money represents to two different individuals that can be problematic.

Money and material items might equate to love and affection for some. For others, they could represent the difference between dependency and control or between safety and instability. If she grew up in a family that exchanged expensive presents as signs of love and affection, she might expect to get the same treatment from a partner in adulthood. But suppose you were raised to believe working hard, saving money, and providing a stable home environment meant love and affection? You're two people who both mean well, but don't be surprised when you bump heads.

3. *Despite our differences, how can we create and commit to shared financial goals?*

Here's where having a "So what? Now what?" attitude comes in handy. If you're not going to break up over the fact that you're a spender and she's a saver, then it's time to figure out what goals are most important to you, individually and as a couple. If it's too early in the relationship to be considering larger goals together, then create individual goals and hold each other accountable. Now that you know each other's financial strengths and weaknesses, don't use them as tools to condemn one another. Use them to empower each other to be better, do better, and achieve more.

Real TALK

Use each other's financial strengths and weaknesses to empower each other.

HOW DO I RECOGNIZE A WOMAN WHO JUST WANTS ME FOR MY MONEY?

More than the gold-diggers we hear so much about on reality TV, you might need to be concerned about slackers. Just because you want a certain lifestyle, doesn't mean a woman should be able to attach herself to you and enjoy the same lifestyle without doing her part to contribute. For some couple's this means both people bringing home a paycheck, and for others it means one spouse will contribute to the relationship in other ways, such as caring for the home and children. The bottom line is that you shouldn't be expected to be the only one giving in a relationship. And if you're still looking for that lifelong partner, you're perfectly within your rights to have a standard for the income you'd like her to earn or the contributions you'd like her to make to the household. This doesn't mean your woman won't enjoy being wined and dined, as many of us do, but there should always be some giving and receiving on both sides. That's what building a lasting partnership is about.

WHY SHOULDN'T I TAKE CARE OF THE FINANCES WHILE MY WIFE TAKES CARE OF THE HOME?

You cannot be a woman's financial plan. Whether or not your wife works outside of the home, you must both be ready, willing, and able to manage your finances at all times. If you were to become disabled or pass away unexpectedly, a lack of knowledge about your personal finances would make a difficult time much more stressful for your wife. If she doesn't know what accounts you have and how to access them, what bills you have and how to pay them, and what insurance arrangements you have and how to file necessary claims, her grief will be compounded by frustration and a sense of helplessness. Do you really want to risk leaving the woman you love in that position?

WHAT SHOULD I DO IF DISCOVER MY MATE IS FUNDAMENTALLY BAD WITH MONEY?

Well, first of all, don't make yourself sound like a saint or a victim. More likely than not, she didn't become irresponsible this far into the relationship. You either saw the signs and chose to ignore them or failed to have the right conversations with her early on.

I'm not blaming you. I'm encouraging you to take ownership of your part in the situation. Your mate probably showed you her true colors

Real TALK

When people show you who they really are, believe them.

long before diamond rings, a shared home, and cute little babies entered into the picture. (See: *What are the warning signs of a financially irresponsible person?*) As they say, when people show you who they really are, believe them. Accept that you'll never be able to change anyone but yourself.

Now that you're at this place, don't become a jerk about it. Do whatever it takes to set the right mood to have an honest, judgment-free conversation with your honey. (See: *Are there questions I should ask about money while we're dating?*) No matter how difficult the talk is to have, you can't create a truly great relationship until you can openly communicate about this topic. Trust me, once you can talk about money without getting defensive or blowing up, you'll be able to talk about anything.

HOW CAN I MAKE MY LADY BETTER WITH MONEY?

Let's be clear. You really can't *make* anyone but yourself better with money. You can motivate your significant other and encourage her as much as possible, but if you think you can just change her, you better think again!

Real TALK
If you think you can change your woman, think again!

Remember, everyone has their own financial blueprint, and had you taken time to ask the right questions while you were dating, you'd know hers by now. No worries though. Even though she's already officially your woman, it's not too late. Use the steps below to help her manage her money.

1. **GET BACK TO THE BASICS.** If neither of you knows why she interacts with money the way she does, neither of you will be able to help her make progress. Start with the basic questions all couples should know answer for each other. (See: *Are there questions I should ask about money while we're dating?*)

2. **CREATE A SAFE SPACE.** Once you know what her money personality is, don't be judgmental. It's not your job to be her financial godfather, lurking over every purchase or financial decision she makes. Become a resource for her. If she opens up enough to ask you for help, give it freely. Leave all of your putdowns and looks of disgust at the door, no matter how frustrated you are. You promised to help, so be helpful.

3. **WORK AS A TEAM.** If she's willing to acknowledge her money skills could use some fine-tuning, work with her. Offer to help her set up a budget, open the proper bank accounts, hire the right financial professionals, or whatever else she needs. Don't boss her around. Be supportive, and change your mindset from what *she* needs to get done to what *we* need to get done.

4. **LEAD BY EXAMPLE.** When all else fails, keep doing you, if what you're doing is right. If you're notorious for imposing rules you don't follow, then you can forget about getting her on the bandwagon anytime soon. Be the change you would like to see in her. Eventually, she may come around. If she doesn't, you have some tough choices to make.

SHE MAKES MORE MONEY THAN I DO. WHY DOES THAT MAKE ME UNCOMFORTABLE SOMETIMES?

According to a 2012 *USA Today* analysis of the U.S. Census Bureau, in a record 23% of families, women are the primary breadwinners, out-earning their husbands by 28% when both spouses work. This means the wife is bringing home the bacon, or at least more bacon than her husband, in more than 12 million American families.

No woman who loves you will try to make you feel like less of a man because you don't make as much money as she does. If that's the case in your situation, you need to address her behavior and come to an understanding as to how she can improve in that area.

If your wife or girlfriend is handling her success gracefully, then the problem lies with you. Do you feel like you should be earning more? Do you know you should? If so, step up your money game, and do everything in your power to maximize your income. Go back to the "Earn More Money" section of this book, and take action on every point that applies to you. You'll feel a lot more secure when you're earning at your full potential— even if she's still earning more.

EACH TIME MY MATE AND I DISCUSS MONEY, THINGS GET TENSE. HOW CAN WE GET THROUGH THIS?

For the first few years of my marriage, things were tight. Gerald and I had been business partners in the real estate firm, each of us earning well into six figures, since college. By the time we got married, the real estate market was tanking, and we were living off savings. We went from eating out for breakfast, lunch, and dinner to lingering around the house until one of us couldn't take the hunger anymore and broke down and cooked. It was tough.

Real TALK

When it comes to money, compromise can leave you both feeling like losers.

Not only were we dealing with merging our finances, we were each struggling with the fact that we didn't have many finances to manage anymore. It took quite a few sessions of counseling and periods of going at each other's throats for us to realize we were stressed and taking it out on one another. As the pastor administering our couple's counseling reminded us, "When your money becomes funny, so does your honey."

My husband and I have learned:

1. **TIMING IS EVERYTHING.** Early on in our marriage, I wanted to discuss issues when it was convenient for me, which happened to be the moment they came up. If I wanted to call him in the middle of the day about a bill, I would. If I wanted to wake him up in the middle of the night, I would. If I wanted to get something off my chest as soon as he walked through the door, you guessed it. I would. And if he wasn't in the mood to deal with my shenanigans, I felt like he didn't care about our bills, or our credit, or getting out of debt as much as I did.

   Over time, Gerald taught me how to bring things to his attention, and I was willing to learn for the sake of our relationship. Now I know that when he gets home from work, I've got to give him a little time to unwind from the day. Waiting also gives me time to process the situation, so I'm not as emotional. I can present the facts, and we can solve any issues logically and as a team.

2. **COMPROMISE ISN'T BENEFICIAL.** I know it goes against much of what you've probably learned, but when it comes to money, compromise can leave

you both feeling like losers. With this sort of lose-lose solution, neither person gets what they want, and one or both of you ends up feeling cheated. A win-win solution, by contrast, occurs when your way meets her way and creates our way. Get clear about the specific underlying concerns you're both having, and address those. Work together and come up with specific solutions to address each smaller concern that's creating big blowouts over money.

3. **DON'T PLAY THE BLAME GAME.** After you have a huge disagreement about money, you might be tempted to try and figure out who's at fault. Remember you both learned how to interact with money in different ways. Neither of you is wrong, per se, just different. If you use words like, "you should have," or "you're the reason why," you're not actually trying to resolve the issue. You're aggravating the situation by making the other person feel defensive.

Instead of blaming your partner for what's not working, look back at your own behavior and ask yourself what you can do differently in the future. It's not your job or your right to decide what your partner should do differently. Focus on your own behavior. Start telling your partner, "Next time, I think I could," and see how that changes the tone of the conversation.

HOW DO WE DECIDE WHO SHOULD MANAGE THE MONEY?

When I got heavily into real estate in my early twenties, most of the clients I served were older than I was by ten, twenty, or even thirty years. I can't tell you how many stories I heard from women who didn't know how to manage their money because they'd always depended on a husband to do it and he was no longer there. If you love the woman in your life, you don't want to leave her in that position.

The key is to look at your family like a team, with each person playing his or her own position while working toward a common goal. Gerald and I recognized early on that managing our family's finances was my strength. For his part, he does all the family shopping, all the travel planning, and the planning for major events. If he tries to step in to play my position, or vice versa, the team falls apart, and we both lose. At the same time, we keep each other informed of how things are going in our individual areas of responsibility. If anything ever happens to one of us, we each know how much we spend monthly, the location of savings and investments, and how to access the funds. We sit down and discuss any changes at least once a month, and twice a month we sync our calendars. We also discuss all major purchases, and come up with a game plan for making them.

This has nothing to do with gender. Household money management is a shared task with more responsibility leaning toward whoever is naturally better at handling the money. If you both suck at it, you're going to have to choose the person that sucks less, keep the lines of communication open, and get help. (See: *What professionals should I have on my financial team?*)

MY WIFE IS A STAY-AT-HOME MOM. DOES SHE HAVE TO BE INVOLVED WITH THE FINANCES?

Stay-at-home mom is not an easy job. It requires long hours of hard work. In addition, having one spouse stay home and care for the kids can save your family thousands of dollars every year on transportation, child care, clothing, dry cleaning, and more.

Regardless of the savings, this is the arrangement you two agreed upon—at least it should be—so don't try to play her like staying at home somehow makes her incapable of, or undeserving of, having a voice in your family's finances. And don't let her get away with saying you can just handle the money either. It's in everyone's best interest for her to take on her share of responsibility in the way that works best for you two. At the very least, she should have basic knowledge of your debts, assets, bills, and bank accounts.

(See: *How do we decide who should manage the money?*)

SHOULD COUPLES SHARE BANK ACCOUNTS?

Well, let's get the obvious out of the way. If you're not married, you definitely should not merge bank accounts or open a joint account. If you are married, I believe it's a matter of personal preference, but I heard a divorce attorney put it this way. "It's easier for a divorce if you keep your money separate, but it's better for a marriage if everything's in one pot."

When I coach couples occasionally, I recommend a His, Hers, and Ours bank account method. As suggested by the names, the couple creates one joint account that serves as a mutual money melting pot for household bills and other expenses, such as groceries and dry cleaning. This method may also extend to a second account, which houses joint savings for long-term goals like vacations, or home renovations.

While joint accounts may be a great test of your patience, they can foster transparency and build trust, as long as each spouse communicates and respects the agreed upon boundaries for use of those funds.

> **$ Real MONEY**
>
> Agreeing with your partner to maintain minimum balances in your joint accounts can make you both more comfortable.

In the His and Hers accounts, each spouse basically gets predetermined fun money they can do anything with—no questions asked. If the husband wants to golf with his buddies, he should be able to do so free of judgment, as long as the household expenses are handled. The same goes for the wife. A night out with the girls or a day of pampering at the local spa shouldn't become a blown out of proportion "discussion" simply because either party disagrees with how their spouse unwinds.

Joint accounts or not, there has to be open communication about what's going on. I teach my clients to treat the process like a business deal, free of emotions. If two companies merge, everyone has to start out on equal footing. Terms have to be agreed upon, and each partner should be fully aware of how accounts will be used.

DO YOU SUGGEST I KEEP A SECRET STASH MY PARTNER KNOWS NOTHING ABOUT?

I get asked this question more than you'd guess. While I completely understand the thinking behind it, and would be a complete liar if I said it hadn't crossed my mind in the early days of my relationship, it saddens me.

Hiding money, while encouraged by well-meaning friends and protective parents, is the bedrock of mistrust in a marriage. While it may feel like you have one up on the other person, you both lose when this secret stash eventually comes to light.

Hiding money doesn't help you solve the real problem at hand, which is that you either don't believe your wife is capable of sound money management or you don't believe the relationship will last. Both scenarios are embedded in deeper issues that don't disappear because you've got a few dollars tucked away.

If you feel the urge to stash money because you think your wife will blow every last penny of the family funds, then there are several other steps you need to take. As you learned earlier in this chapter, lack of communication is the leading cause of divorce. In a non-threatening way, have a conversation about what financial thresholds make you comfortable and uncomfortable. For example, you may not like the checking or savings account to dip below a certain dollar amount. Explain this to her, and work together to come up with ways you can both contribute to keep balances above the agreed upon minimum. If circumstances require a change to these standards, make sure the decision is reached mutually, so no one feels left out or guilty.

Real TALK

Secrets are secrets. You can't keep your own hidden stash of money and get mad at her for doing the same.

Realize that your mate had a certain way of doing things way before you came along. While you may believe that if she really cares about you she should, would, and could do what you want her to do, these things take time. I can honestly say it took at least three years for my husband and me to finally find a groove and create an our-way scenario, as opposed to the his-way and my-way methods we tried to force on each other in the beginning.

Ultimately, you're in charge of setting the boundaries you believe will protect you best. I can't define those for you, and neither can anyone else. I encourage you not to forget the Golden Rule: Do unto others as you would have them do unto you. Before you start keeping secrets in your relationship, understand that secrets are secrets. Don't justify yours and then condemn those she may want to keep, including her own hidden stash of money.

AT WHAT POINT SHOULD I ACCEPT THAT THE MONEY ISSUES HAVE COMPLETELY RUINED OUR MARRIAGE?

If your spouse honestly just doesn't get it, then you have some tough decisions to make. As a firm believer that there's hope in many situations, I'm pretty optimistic that with a bit of determination and teamwork, things will work out in your favor. But what happens when you've tried to improve communication, set boundaries, and shared what you know in a loving way, and things still aren't working out?

While my personal belief is that money should be managed collectively, in these extreme scenarios, you may decide to manage your funds separately. That means that while you may chip in on household bills like roommates, you'd be responsible for your own retirement, long-term care, and the like. Be aware, however, that this is a short-term fix. I've seen men who were diligent with their own financial affairs but stayed married to someone who wasn't. When the wife could no longer work or simply created a financial mess, who do you think had to foot the bill?

Where my optimism fizzles, and I prefer to draw a line, is when your partner's mismanagement turns into blatant malice. If you two have debated so much about money that you now harbor resentment toward each other that manifests in nasty ways, it's time to reevaluate the relationship as a whole. If the mismanagement spirals into *intentionally* failing to take care of basic necessities, that's a problem. I've seen men exhaust retirement funds, abuse student loan refund checks, and land in tens of thousands of dollars in credit card debt because of their spouse's selfishness and the man's desire to "be the provider." Again, while I'm a strong proponent of marriage, I'm not tolerant of financial abuse.

My former pastor, Bishop Kenneth C. Ulmer of Faithful Central Bible Church in Inglewood, California, put it best when he said, "People should treat you how you want to be treated—not how they feel like treating you." If your gut tells you that you're being taken advantage of, please don't ignore your intuition because of me or what I've written here or what anyone else says. If you're just hurt and paranoid from a previous situation, that's one thing, but if you truly feel that you cannot trust your future or stability with a person, by all means follow your heart.

You're blessed with gut instinct for a reason. Sure, there are times that your wires may get a bit crossed, but the danger lies in failing to listen to your inner voice and allowing a woman or a relationship to completely override your good judgment. If your instincts have you constantly concerned about what your mate will do financially and how it will impact you, embrace that feeling and address it. If it's a misunderstanding, then it should be easily resolved through counseling or by using the communication tips discussed throughout the section. If you're still concerned, you have to decide if the relationship is worth the risk.

HOW DO I RECOVER FINANCIALLY AFTER A DIVORCE OR BREAK UP?

You'll never recondition what you don't recognize. Be honest with yourself.

While most news reports focus on the struggles of single mothers after a divorce, the financial setback following the breakup of a marriage can be just as tough on men. While a number of issues may arise in a divorce, from stress to low self-esteem and depression, a lack of financial resources, new obligations like spousal support and child support, and ignorance of the concepts of how to manage money add insult to injury.

Consider these steps as you work to heal both emotionally and financially.

1. **GET CLEAR ABOUT YOUR ROLE.** Be honest with yourself. If you're in a financial mess, what did you do, or not do, that contributed to the matter? Did you participate in frivolous spending so the two of you could "live the life?" Did you go along to get along when you knew you should have put your foot down? Were you okay with not knowing what she was doing with her money and credit cards?

   You'll never recondition what you don't first recognize. Once you acknowledge your part, you can figure out how to avoid the same type of destructive behavior in the future. The last thing you want to do is repeat the exact same pattern with a brand new person.

2. **GET EDUCATED ON WHERE YOU STAND FINANCIALLY.** Once you have a clear picture of how you ended up where you are, don't let guilt get the best of

YOUR HONEY, YOUR MONEY

you. Don't waste time beating yourself up. The real work to get your money right begins now.

Start by creating a budget based on your new solo income and any new financial obligations, such as new child care expenses, travel expenses to see your children or to bring them to you, or court-ordered child support, spousal support, or buy-out payments. (See: *How do I know if I've created a realistic budget?*) Next, pull your credit report at www.annualcredit-report.com. Make sure everything you see is actually something you recognize as your debt. If your ex has any fraudulent activity going on, you're going to need to address it ASAP. (See: *What should I do if there are items on my credit report I don't recognize?*) If it's all yours, add it up, and create your plan for debt elimination. (See: *What is a debt eliminator, and how do I determine my debt-free date?*)

3. **GET PROFESSIONAL HELP.** Look into no-cost or low-cost consumer credit counseling in your area by visiting the National Foundation for Credit Counseling at www.nfcc.org. You want to find a counselor that can help you set realistic financial goals and get a sound plan in place to meet your unique needs at this delicate stage of life.

————153————

FRIENDS & FAMILY OR FINANCIAL FOES

LITTLE BOYS LEARN EARLY on that they're expected to grow up to be providers, but when did that come to mean you're responsible for and take care of *everybody* from adult children to godchildren you haven't seen in years to your boy who's out of work and needs a loan to make his rent?

The inability to have much needed conversations about money extends well beyond the romantic realm. I don't know very many people who haven't been asked to loan a loved one money or to take on some financial responsibility for a friend or family member at some point. From picking up the tab for a friend who's not working, but still insists on going out every weekend, to covering a payment for your first cousin who keeps forgetting his car payment is due at the same time every month, you've likely been faced with, or will be faced with, a request to financially aid someone close to you. While you may find this noble, if you're not careful, it can eventually affect you negatively. You can give to the point you have nothing left to meet your own basic needs. And if you're riddled with debt and don't have adequate savings, you're on a slippery slope that can potentially leave you broke, no matter how well you attempt to manage your finances.

✅AFFIRM

I deserve and enjoy the finer things in life.

There are many instances in which you may believe you're helping, and every once in a while, perhaps you are. But when you allow another grown individual to become a line item on your struggling monthly budget, you have to ask yourself who you're really helping and who you're hurting. As singer, actor, and author, Tyrese Gibson once shared in a discussion, "Sometimes to help someone, you have to stop helping them." Learn to empower, not enable. Don't turn friends and family into financial foes.

HOW CAN I TELL IF I'M FINANCIALLY ENABLING SOMEONE?

"Sometimes, to help someone, you have to stop helping them."

If there's even a thought in your mind that you might be enabling someone, you probably are. But to be 100% clear, an enabler is one that enables another to achieve an end; especially one who enables another to persist in self-destructive behavior (such as substance abuse) by providing excuses or by making it possible to avoid the consequences of such behavior.

Before you move on feeling some sense of superiority, please note that while the definition cites substance abuse as a self-destructive behavior, it doesn't disqualify those that financially enable friends and family. It's one thing to assist someone who finds himself or herself in a bind from time to time, but it's another to add their needs to your monthly expenses. Not only is this kind of helping actually hurting them, but it can be hurting you, as well.

Listen, I know how it feels to think you're obligated to assist family and friends. After all, isn't it the manly thing to do? It might be, if it weren't for the fact that this kind behavior often creates an inability in people to figure things out on their own. Dependence on you can prevent them from learning how to earn their own income and manage their own money wisely, how to distinguish between their wants and needs, how to hustle, and how to pay their bills on time.

So how can you tell if you're enabling someone in your life? Answer yes or no to the following questions.

1. Do you constantly find yourself having to bail out grown and able-bodied adults? (If you're a parent and your "baby" is above college-age, yes, they count as an adult.)

2. Do you tell the few people who actually offer to pay you back not to worry about it?

3. Do you financially support anyone whose neediness is purely derived out of their own laziness?

4. Do you find yourself worried about this person, or convinced that he or she can't handle basic life situations without falling apart?

5. Do you excuse this person's behavior as a result of the economy, stress, misunderstanding, or difficulty coping, even when the behavior hurts or inconveniences you?

6. Do you feel like you have a unique and special relationship with this person, unlike anyone else they may know?

7. Do you feel protective of this person, even though he or she is an adult and is capable of taking care of his or her life?

8. Do you wish others in this person's life would change their behavior or attitudes to make things easier for this person?

9. Do you feel reluctant to refer this individual to a source of help or assistance because you doubt that anyone else can understand the situation the way you do?

10. Do you ever feel manipulated by this person but ignore your feelings to avoid conflict?

11. Do you make yourself available to another person at the expense of your own financial obligations, energy, or time?

12. Do you hear from others that you're too close to this person or the situation?

Real need inspires real motivation.

If you thought "yes," reluctantly grunted your agreement, bit your lower lip, or tried to explain to yourself why your case is different, then more than likely you, my friend, are an enabler.

Here's how you can stop enabling those you claim to love.

1. **STOP ENABLING AND START EMPOWERING.** There's an old, yet relevant Chinese proverb which says, "Give a man a fish, and you'll feed him for a day, but if you teach a man to fish, you'll feed him for a lifetime."

   Don't take away a person's ability to hustle. The fact of the matter is that you won't always be around to go fishing for them. If you keep enabling them, they'll starve once they have to go it on their own. Do you really want to leave someone you care about without basic money survival skills?

   Remember, *real need inspires real motivation.* People will not learn to be responsible as long as they know they'll always have you as a backup plan.

2. **INSTEAD OF REACHING IN YOUR WALLET, REFER THOSE IN NEED TO COMMUNITY RESOURCES AND SERVICES.** Your constant helping tells them, "I support your self-destructive and negative behavior so much I'm going to give you more money, so you can keep it going."

   Actions speak louder than words. You can give the inspirational "get your life together" speeches all day, you can get angry and swear before the Almighty that this is the last time you'll help, but what you *do* is always speaking so much more loudly than what you *say.*

3. **TAKE YOU OUT OF THEIR PROBLEMS.** This is not about *you* being an awesome person. This is not about *you* doing your good deed so you can make it through those pearly gates. In fact, this isn't about *you* at all. This is about each person figuring out life on his or her own.

   If nothing else, remember that the money you continue to dole out to irresponsible friends and family members could be used to get yourself out of debt, buy your first home, or save for your retirement. There's nothing selfish about considering yourself every once in a while. After all, the folks you're enabling definitely don't care about you or your future, and believe me, when your money runs out and you have nothing else to give, they'll just move on to the next overly generous enabler.

HOW DOES CO-SIGNING A LOAN FOR SOMEONE ELSE AFFECT ME?

When you co-sign for a loan, you basically tell the lender that you accept equal responsibility for the loan's repayment. You're guaranteeing that if the borrower fails to pay, you'll make the payment!

Real MONEY

When you co-sign, you're promising to pay the debt if the borrower doesn't.

You're not just helping your friend or family member get a loan. You're literally promising that you'll pay the debt yourself if the borrower doesn't. Studies have shown that as many as three out of four co-signers (75%) ultimately end up making payments on the loan.

So what happens if you co-sign on a loan and the borrower defaults?

1. If the lender decides to sue and actually wins, your wages can be garnished or liens and judgments can be placed against your personal property until the debt is satisfied.

2. Your credit report can be severely tarnished from several months of late payments, as well as a judgment against you.

UN REAL

75% of co-signers ultimately end up making loan payments.

3. You may eventually have to pay up to the full amount of the debt, in addition to late fees or collection costs.

If for some reason none of the above scares you, and you're still considering co-signing for a friend or relative, please *always* remember these tips.

1. **KNOW THE PERSON YOU'RE ATTEMPTING TO HELP.** Before agreeing to sign on the dotted line, study the person's financial habits and make sure you're comfortable with his or her money-management skills.

2. **VERIFY THAT PERSON'S EMPLOYMENT AND TAKE HOME PAY BY REVIEWING PAYCHECK STUBS AND BANK STATEMENTS.** If the borrower doesn't want to share that type of personal information, he shouldn't be asking you to put your credit worthiness in jeopardy.

3. **UNDERSTAND YOUR OWN ABILITY TO PAY.** Make sure you have enough income left over each month to pay the minimum payment on this account should the borrower fail to pay.

4. **BE SURE YOU HAVE AN OPPORTUNITY TO DISCUSS ALL OF THE TERMS OF THE AGREEMENT WITH THE LENDER.** This is your loan just as much as it is the borrower's. Know all the details of what you're getting into.

If you feel uncertain about one or more of the above points, do not co-sign. Think about the reason this person can't qualify for a loan on his or her own. There's good cause for why the bank isn't willing to take on that risk. Protecting your credit is up to you!

SHOULD I LEND MONEY TO FRIENDS?

Real MONEY

Never lend money you can't afford to give away.

Never lend money that you can't afford to give. Loaning money to your friends, or even family, is a really bad decision when you're not truly in a position to do so. If you want to lend money to someone in need, you may as well as consider it a gift and let go of any expectation that you'll get the money back. If they repay you, great! If they don't, then there should be no love lost, because your primary concern was helping them out, and you did just that.

The problem with some folks is that they keep coming back once they realize how generous you are. During college, I was mentored by author and comedian Steve Harvey, who always says, "The best thing you can do for a poor person is *not* become one of them." I wholeheartedly agree. Learn now to say *no*, and teach your friends and family members how to do just what you're learning how to do—take *personal* responsibility for their *personal* finances.

If you decide to lend money to someone, at least take a few precautionary steps to help protect your interests.

1. Be clear about what the money is for, and be sure there are no alternatives you can help the borrower come up with before you reach into your own pocket.

2. Put the terms in writing, so all parties involved understand that this is a loan and not a gift.

3. Set up a repayment plan with a firm due date. Either agree to accept a realistic number of equal installments or determine a date when all funds should be made payable. Outline the consequences for non-payment.

4. If possible, make sure the agreement is made with someone else present as a witness.

5. Always leave a paper trail. Exchange funds via money order, cashier's check, or personal check. Never give cash.

6. Please reconsider, and don't lend money!

Seem cumbersome? Great! It's designed to. Hopefully, you'll require so much the person wanting to borrow money would rather take their sob stories and broken promises elsewhere.

WHAT'S WRONG WITH BORROWING MONEY FROM MY FRIENDS OR RELATIVES EVERY ONCE IN A WHILE?

Unless we're talking about borrowing $25 or less until you can find your misplaced debit card, you absolutely should not borrow money from people. I'm not really a fan of lending money, but I'm even less of a fan of borrowing. What your friends and family probably don't have the heart to tell you is that they see you as "that person."

Yes, you're the one they avoid at all costs, because they know borrowing money is a way of life for you. They don't want to tell you they wish you'd get it together and stop treating them as if they're your personal ATM, or even worse, as if their opportunity fund is your opportunity fund. Is that clear enough? Good. Tell them to thank me later.

Listen, I'm not trying to "shame you to death," as my granny would say, but someone has to tell you. Unless we're dealing with extremely unique and unusual circumstances, you shouldn't borrow money, especially if you don't earn a consistent income and can't commit to a solid plan for repayment. Do you think your friends and family members can honestly afford to just give you money? I know you said "borrow," but if they lend to you, more than likely they'll end up having to accept that they gave you the money, or you'll lose the relationship all together.

Don't put your loved ones in an awkward position. Borrowing money makes relationships tricky. If you're truly in a bind and your friend loans you money, the first time he sees you with something that even remotely looks new, he'll think to herself, "That dude owes me money, but he's got a new watch?" I say, just avoid this altogether. Don't borrow from people who genuinely mean something to you, and if, despite everything I've said, you feel you have to ask to borrow money, don't be mad when folks turn you down.

HOW DO I DEAL WITH FRIENDS WHO ARE WAY AHEAD OF ME IN THE MONEY GAME?

Much of the debt my clients find themselves in comes from buying stuff they really didn't need in the first place, like shoes, expensive vacations, wide screen televisions, home improvements, tickets to sporting events and concerts, and expensive cars. When we get to the root of why they make purchases they don't need and can't afford, those that are honest typically mention a close friend, family member, or neighbor who had something the client wanted.

It's natural to be attracted to things a friend already has, but that doesn't mean you should try to keep up with his lifestyle, especially when he's in a totally different tax bracket. It's more than possible to maintain a wonderful friendship, and remain understanding and respectful of each other's circumstances.

Use these strategies to deal with friends that may not share your financial struggles.

1. **DON'T TRY TO KEEP UP!** Just because your friends can travel four times a year, doesn't mean you should attempt to do the same. Be realistic about what you can spend, otherwise you'll run yourself into debt trying to figure out how to keep up with someone who may be doing this effortlessly, or who may be worse off than you are, despite his Oscar-worthy performance as the man with the money.

2. **DON'T MAKE THEM FEEL GUILTY.** If you see your friends spending what you believe is "too much money," don't chastise them or attempt to make them feel guilty. At the same time, don't expect them to always pick up the tab just because they have, or seem to have, more money than you.

3. **MAKE SUGGESTIONS THAT WORK FOR YOU.** If your friends aren't bound by the same budgetary constraints you are, they may suggest you bond over a last minute trip to Las Vegas or $500 concert seats. Even if you don't want to go into tons of details about your own situation, don't be afraid to suggest alternative hang-out options. You can search for the best cheap eats in your town, tell them you're not up for travel the moment, or look for deals on tickets to events that fit your budget.

4. **RETURN THE FAVOR ON YOUR TERMS.** If your wealthier friends start to pick up on the fact that your wallet is a little lighter than theirs, they may want to treat you more when you go out. It's normal to want to reciprocate, but you'll obviously have to figure out ways to return the favour within your means. Instead of picking up the dinner tab, buy a round of drinks or find other less expensive ways to hold up your end of the friendship.

5. **USE ANY NEGATIVE FEELINGS FOR GOOD.** Understand that any feelings of jealousy you may experience are completely normal. Find a way to make those emotions work for you. Use them to motivate you to accomplish your own financial goals as quickly as possible. Turn the pain into a greater purpose.

Most importantly, never forget to keep things in perspective. You never know what financial situation a person may truly be in. Many people appear to rolling in money, but you have no idea what they may be going through to keep up appearances.

I THINK MY FRIENDS ARE TAKING ADVANTAGE OF ME FINANCIALLY. HOW DO I PROTECT MYSELF, BUT KEEP THE FRIENDSHIPS?

I hate to be the one to break this to you, but if there are people taking advantage of you financially, or in any other manner, they're really not your friends. By the time you've gotten to the point of asking this question, you know who your real friends are.

If you have friends, male or female, that expect you to help them out financially because they think you can, make them aware of the problem. Ask them plainly if they're only hanging around you because of your ability to pay for things, or is it because they truly enjoy your company. A true friend will understand your need for clarification and respect you for bringing the subject up for discussion.

Understand there are two parties in this type of co-dependent relationship: the used and the user. You're allowing yourself to be used. Think about why you continue to befriend a person who only wants to take advantage of you. Are you lonely to some extent? Is it hard for you to make friends for some reason? Do you feel like the only thing you bring to the table is your paycheck? Do you like feeling like the hero no matter what the costs?

Everybody recognizes that guy at the bar who's always buying rounds for everyone, or the one who picks up the check every time you go out to dinner, whether or not he's in the financial position to do so. Most of us can see he's trying to prove his self-worth by spending his money on people. For whatever reason, he feels the need to buy the friendship and approval of the people around him. At some point in his life, that kind of behavior must've worked, or seemed to work, and now it's become a habit.

Maybe you don't see yourself in those examples, but if you're lending money to people all the time, even though you can't afford it, you may be in the same position. In either situation, you have to uncover and acknowledge the root of this problem, and it doesn't begin with your friends. It begins with understanding your own value as an individual. You don't need to buy friendships or approval, and spending or lending when you can't afford to isn't heroic.

Take money out of these friendships. Don't lend anyone money or offer to purchase anything for them. Keep conversations pertaining to money to a minimum, or eliminate them altogether. Take note of your friends' reactions when you have no money to offer, and see how long they stick around. Those that still show up and continue to invest in your relationship are actual friends. The others don't deserve your friendship, and you should be more discriminating in who you choose to call "friend" in the future.

HOW DO I FIND THE COURAGE TO SAY *NO* TO A LOVED ONE THAT NEEDS HELP?

It's amazing that *no* seems to be the hardest word for many of us to say out loud. Strangely, it seems easier to say, "Of course, I can!" or "No problem!" or "I'll be glad to!" Even as you agree, you know you don't want to do whatever it is, and furthermore, you can't afford to do it.

To protect your money, relearn how to say "no" with the enthusiasm of a two-year-old.

In order to say *no* to requests that will negatively affect your finances, you have to relearn how to say *no* with the same enthusiasm as the average two-year-old. After plenty of spankings and redirections from adults, toddlers finally give in and drop *no* from their vocabulary. Instead, many of us substitute lots of ways to be agreeable and keep other people happy, even to our own detriment. People-pleasing is a learned behavior.

You know the difference between people who constantly find themselves in sticky situations because of the poor choices they make and people dealing with an unfortunate circumstance beyond their control. Deep down, you also know which of those people will never get it together. At least they won't as long as you continue to intervene on their behalf.

In the *Mindset + Money Master Class*®, I remind participants often that we're each blessed with unique gifts, talents, and skills we can use to earn more money. Those gifts are given to us freely, but it's our responsibility to choose whether or not we'll cultivate and use them. When we don't, we may suffer unnecessarily, not just in our finances, but also emotionally and spiritually.

Real TALK

Don't feel guilty about putting your own needs and wants before someone else's need and want to borrow your money.

When you continuously rescue people from the consequences of their own behavior, you handicap them. You become an obstacle on the journey to uncovering the God-given gifts that could change their lives and their destinies. In all your efforts to help, you hurt them in a way that will have lasting effects. The same source which sustains you can sustain them, but only if you'll get out of the way.

I SAID *NO*, AND NOW MY LOVED ONE ISN'T SPEAKING TO ME. WHAT NEXT?

AFFIRM

I am surrounded by loving, loyal, and solid relationships.

First, let me tell you what's *not* next: giving in again. When you finally decide to say *no* to a repeat offender, embrace the fact that you've chosen your personal finances over someone else's. You deserve to make your desire to save money, pay off debt, and send your children to college debt-free the highest priorities for the money you work hard to earn. Don't be guilted into feeling bad about putting your needs and your wants before someone else's need and want to borrow your money. Being a man doesn't mean taking care of everyone else to the detriment of your personal financial well-being.

Some people will only come into your life for a reason or a season. Whether you're dealing with a close friend or a beloved family member, you have to embrace the gift of goodbye. Not everyone will travel with you to the next phase of your financial transformation. Being in your life is a privilege, and not everyone deserves that privilege, especially those that choose to be angry with you because you're finally ready to make your dreams a reality.

This may seem harsh, but leaving someone behind doesn't have to mean you never speak to them again, unless they're truly toxic. It means you now define for yourself if and how you'll allow them to utilize your time, energy, and resources.

Ask yourself a critical question: *Where are the ships in my life taking me?*

Ships are designed to take people places. If your relation(ship) or friend(ship) isn't taking you anywhere, but is constantly taking away from you, it may be time to abandon ship.

KIDS & MONEY

FINANCIAL EDUCATION OUGHT TO be a mandatory class in every high school, college, and university just as much as biology, algebra, or any other core class, but we've yet to see this happen. Until we wake up as a nation and take a united stance to make it so, teaching our kids about money is still up to us. Despite knowing this, parents are still more likely to talk with their kids about manners, grades, eating habits, drugs and alcohol, and the risks of smoking than about managing money wisely.

The New Living Translation of Proverbs 19:18 says, "Discipline your children while there is hope. If you don't, you will ruin their lives." Whether your child is two years old or thirty-two years old, you still play a very important role in how they interact with money. At any stage, you have the power to handicap them for life or to help them harness a strong sense of financial stability.

Instilling financial discipline is easiest at a young age, especially if you can do it in an engaging and practical way that will make wealthy habits come naturally. Maybe your "little ones" are fully grown adults, and you've spent the majority of their lives enabling them. Don't worry. As long as there's still breath in your body, it's not too late to turn it around.

If your children are still minors, remember those little cuties won't be kids forever. If you want to break some generational curses and cycles, you've got some tough decisions to make. And you better make them quickly, because your kids and your money are both depending on you.

HOW CAN I MAKE SURE MY YOUNG CHILDREN HAVE FUN LEARNING ABOUT MONEY?

The best way to encourage conscientious spending habits in your children is to exhibit those habits every day.

Teaching children about money doesn't have to be difficult. Younger children are so eager to learn all they can and be more adult-like that they're willing to try anything once, especially if it's interesting. I find the clients that have the most problems sharing financial concepts with their children struggle because they're battling their own issues with money. In order to really help your children, you've got to get over any fear of not being perfect with money and remember you definitely know more than enough to start teaching a child.

Here are a few to ideas get you started.

1. USE CASH WHEN POSSIBLE.

There's no minimum age on being a smart saver and conscious spender, but showing younger kids how to budget and spend through the use of a credit or debit card won't do much good. More often than not it's too abstract for a young mind. A child is more likely to equate a card with an endless supply of resources on the other end. Kids need to see money, and see it leaving your hand in exchange for something else, as much as possible. This teaches them that most things in life come at a cost and when the money is gone, it's really gone. Start with something as simple as allowing small children to deposit coins in a parking meter or occasionally paying for your purchases in cash.

While younger children may have trouble grasping the concept of off-site savings, they have no problem with a piggy bank for their coins and a wallet for dollars. As soon as they're old enough to count, encourage them to periodically add up their money and see how much they've saved. The physical action of putting the money back in the piggy bank or wallet will teach them that they don't have to spend every dollar they have and that saving is encouraged and absolutely normal. As their savings grow, remind them of what they had at last count and what they have now. Don't forget to continuously praise them for being great savers.

2. USE PRACTICAL, EVERYDAY SCENARIOS.

The best way to encourage conscientious spending habits is to exhibit them in everyday life. When you plan a trip to the grocery store, get small children involved in making the list. Make sticking to it a game. They ask for something extra, but your goal is to teach them to avoid a would-be saver's biggest obstacle: impulse buying. Tell them the dollar amount you wish to spend (your budget) upfront and make hitting the number or coming in below it a high-five moment at the checkout stand.

You can also help little ones set goals early. Start with small things like books or small toys that cost less than $10. Challenge them to do extra tasks around the house to earn money, so they can buy the item on their own. When they reach their goals, congratulate them and encourage them to set an even larger goals. Help them search online for an item they'd like to buy that costs around $25. The goal is to teach them patience and planning. The sooner your child learns delayed gratification the better. Print out a picture of the item that includes the price, so they can keep it in a safe place near their piggy bank or wallet. When they're tempted to do something else with their money, this will serve as a great reminder of their goal.

For more worthy and ambitious long-term goals, consider matching grants. For example, you can offer to give them $1 for every $5 they save toward the purchase. This will reward your child's savings discipline.

3. USE BOTH PHYSICAL AND DIGITAL GAMES.

Don't forget old school board games the family can play together. You might be surprised by how the games you remember from childhood have been modernized. Take Monopoly for instance. According to the description of Monopoly's Electronic Banking edition, "It's all about flash, not cash." Players use bank cards instead of paper money. Take a look at my favorite, The Game of Life. The 2007 Twists & Turns version uses a Visa Game Card instead of cash and allows you to determine how many years you'll play before determining who's become most successful after assessing assets and liabilities.

With today's technology, there you'll find plenty of ways to make learning about money fun for kids of all ages. The Internet is full of age-specific money games for kids. Start by checking your financial institution's website. Many banks and credit unions have created fun videos and games to teach kids about money. They make the topic of money entertaining for kids, and they can be used to create an open and interesting family discussion. They also provide backup for what you're already teaching, so you're not always the one preaching about money. You can look for money games on a number of trusted sites online, like www.pbs.org and www.kids.usa.gov.

WHEN AND HOW DO I GIVE MY CHILDREN AN ALLOWANCE?

Real TALK

Children should earn money, just as adults do.

According to the online resource *Kids Money*, the average parent who pays their child an allowance begins when the child is around seven years old.

Most money experts agree that children should be *given* an allowance in order to learn financial skills. I disagree. Children should *earn* money, just as we do. Either way, the conversations you have about what to do with the money are essential to ensuring your children become fiscally responsible.

Why do I believe your kids should earn the money? A majority of the students I meet as I speak around the country understand that they're in college to become productive citizens who earn a living. Unfortunately, many of them have no idea how the whole process works. Why? Because they've been *given* money their entire lives for things they should technically do anyway, like be respectful, clean their bedrooms, empty the trash, and earn good grades. On top of all that, they receive annual raises for simply getting older. When's the last time you got a raise for keeping a tidy office, showing up to work on time, or having a birthday?

Here's the deal with paying your kids for meeting their basic obligations. Once they have other streams of income, like a part-time job or birthday money from grandma, they'll draw a blank when you expect them to do chores at home. Why should they clean up for you when they already have money?

Instead, they need to know basic household chores are just their contribution to the family. It goes like this:

I feed you. You do the dishes.
I drive you to school. You wash my car. You walk around my house. You vacuum.
You asked for a little brother or sister. I gave you one. Now, you babysit.

See where I'm going with this?

Now, any task over and beyond basic household chores is where the earning potential comes into the picture. As parents we take on the burden of having to get so many things done in any given week. What can your kids help with? Need someone to file papers? Do you need a closet or drawer organized? Get creative. We know kids need money, but how can you teach them a valuable lesson and get both parties' needs met?

Many parents implement an allowance with no expectation for how the child should manage the money. In the real world, we don't earn a paycheck and still have the luxury of someone else paying our household bills and covering all of our necessities. That was the point of earning the money.

Parents are responsible for the basics, but kids who earn money should become responsible for the frills. Let me tell you how my mom did it. We'd discuss upfront how much she believed something should cost. If what I wanted went over that amount, I was responsible for the balance *and* the taxes!

Talk about lessons that last a lifetime. After a few embarrassments at checkout registers, this method quickly taught me how fast money could go when I was buying things just to keep up with the Joneses. After every trip to the mall, my mom was fine. She spent only what she wanted to spend. Nothing more. No hard feelings—on her part, at least.

Maybe your children have cell phones on your plan. You want them to be able to call you in case of an emergency, but they should be required to earn the money to pay for the extras, such as texting and accessories. That's not for you! It's to stay in constant touch with their friends. If your children are of driving age, teach them the responsibilities of driving by having them pay for gas every other week or by requiring them to contribute money for auto insurance. My mom added me to her gas card, but I was responsible for the bill from the time I was a senior in high school until I was a senior in college and had to get my own card. Think that helped me cut down on my generous offers to give every friend a ride? Yes, it did.

The important thing to realize here is that allowance is fine, but it needs to come with conditions. You're not going to traumatize your kids by teaching them how to be responsible with money. What are you protecting them from? Real life? They need to know the importance of living beneath their means, giving, and saving. If you wait until they're leaving for college to get the conversation started, you're missing an essential part of the job of preparing them for adulthood.

I THINK I MAY HAVE ENTITLED CHILDREN.
CAN THIS BE CHANGED?

Children lean to be responsible or entitled according to which attitude is rewarded.

As parents, we want to see our children grow up with more opportunities and access than we may have had. That's understandable. What's not understandable, however, is raising children who believe they're due something in life simply because they're breathing. Being responsible, understanding the value of money, and expecting that privileges are to be earned rather than given, are all character traits far too difficult to teach with words, or we'd all memorize a few magical phrases and have perfect children.

While both parents can contribute to this problem of entitlement, I've noticed that fathers tend to have more trouble saying no to their daughters. Remember you don't want your baby girl to grow up thinking she should depend on a man for money. One day, that man won't be you, and his motives might not be as loving as yours.

Answer the following questions to determine whether what you're sensing in your child is a true sense of entitlement.

1. WHAT HAVE YOU BEEN REWARDING?

We learn to be responsible or entitled according to which attitude is rewarded. To teach responsibility, work and accomplishments must be rewarded. To teach entitlement, something else is rewarded. Training a child to be entitled is a very easy task. As parents, we do it constantly by rewarding children for merely existing. We don't require that they demonstrate consistent behavior before we give privileges. You can do what you want with your money, but it's not beneficial to give more money just because the child has reached a certain age. That type of thinking assumes a child will automatically demonstrate responsible behavior as a result of growing older. Often the expectation that the child act responsibly is lost, and the only requirements for reward are being born and having another birthday.

2. HAVE YOU USED YOUR CHILD TO DISPLAY YOUR OWN LEVEL OF SUCCESS?

Some parents do this by giving their children privileges earlier than their stage of development warrants. Ever see a five-year-old in the mall with a cell phone? Or the fourteen-year-old who can't drive, but gets a brand new BMW for her birthday? Could you expect a child with these types of privileges to *not* feel entitled? What could a child in either scenario honestly do to deserve these extravagant and age-inappropriate gifts? The answer is nothing. Please note these are not rewards. They are unearned privileges. This is about the parent wanting to look or feel rich, not about what's actually in the best interest of the child's long-term growth and maturity.

3. ARE YOU MOST CONCERNED WITH YOUR CHILD'S HAPPINESS?

If your main goal in parenting has been to make the world a perfect, pleasant, and constantly happy place for your child at all costs, then you must acknowledge the role you've played in creating this false sense of entitlement. Wanting your kids to have things easier than you did can lead to what's known as the "entitlement model of parenting."

4. DO THE FOLLOWING BELIEFS RESONATE WITH YOU?
   a) Children deserve and have the right to be happy all the time.
   b) Parents need to protect their child from experiencing natural consequences that result from irresponsible behavior. For example, it's okay to lift a restriction and allow the child to attend a practice, so he or she can play in the game on Saturday.
   c) The only way to judge a child's responsibility level is to listen to what the child says or promises he or she will do in the future.
   d) When children reach a particular age, they have rights to certain privileges. If they demonstrate incompetence after the right is given, the right can be taken away and the child will understand that he or she should now work for what previously was given for nothing.

If you agreed with any of those statements, you should know that what you teach an entitled child is that they should be rewarded for existing. This leads them to the following conclusions.

It's your duty to teach your child responsibility.

- *My life should consist of the pursuit of happiness, pleasure, and fun.*
- *You owe me what I need to have a pleasant, fun life.*
- *I can and should be angry when I'm asked to do something to earn what I believe is owed to me.*
- *I can and should be angry when privileges are taken away, because they belong to me.*

With beliefs like those, the entitled child is usually lazy and often belligerent. They don't feel it's necessary to plan ahead or consider others when making plans. An entitled child has no understanding of the fact that their own behavior can result in positive or negative consequences. The entitled child often says things like: *everybody else is doing it, it's their fault, that's not fair, I need,* and most often, *I want.*

Sound familiar?

I hope not, but if it does, understand that if your child isn't learning what you want him or her to learn, it's up to you to change that. It's your duty to teach them responsibility.

A responsible person is defined as one who understands that there are consequences for behavior and therefore plans ahead, so the consequences will be pleasant rather than unpleasant. As a parent, you can only judge the child's mastery of responsibility by evaluating the child's behavior.

To teach responsibility requires you to reward a child for accomplished tasks, rather than for expected behavior or future plans and promises. You have to teach children that their own behavior defines their lives. Continuous responsible behavior brings positive rewards, including financial freedom and freedom in many other area of life. Continued irresponsible behavior results in rewards not being given in the first place and may result in their temporary loss when mistakes are made.

For a different result, you must become dedicated to teaching your child that they don't automatically get things just because they exist. As a result, he or she learns to respect and appreciate others' efforts, because they have a personal understanding of what it means to earn something.

Children will also develop a personal sense of empowerment and self-esteem when they know their own behavior determines what they get in life. Children learn to be responsible or entitled over time, depending on which behavior their parents reward. To unlearn either model will also take time. If your child is consistently disrespectful, despite your efforts at parenting, and you find yourself feeling helpless or incompetent in this area, the child has likely developed an attitude of entitlement. To change this you'll have to change your beliefs as a parent, start rewarding your child only after consistently demonstrated positive behavior, and be willing to tolerate your child's unhappiness in the meantime.

YOU REALLY THINK KIDS SHOULD WORK?

Are you serious? You probably don't want to ask the woman who started working unofficially when she was six years old and illegally when she was thirteen. By first grade, my mom would take me with her and farm me out to other departments in the hotel she worked in to do everything from stuff envelopes to organize and alphabetize folders in junky file cabinets. By

Real TALK
You really don't understand the true value of money until you've earned it yourself.

seventh grade, I spent every holiday and vacation from school at another hotel working in the human resources department. I did everything from answer phones to data entry, and by sixteen years old, I had my own office where I screened applicants, completed background checks, and trained newly hired employees. So again, do you really want to ask me this question?

My grandmother used to say, "You really don't understand the true value of money until you've earned it yourself." By encouraging kids to work, parents can effectively teach their children the value of money and help them understand that money really doesn't grow on trees. It's unfortunate, but in this day and age, you'll find college students who aren't sure where money comes from. Remember our chat about entitled children? (See: *I think I may have entitled children. Can this be changed?*)

Allowing your kids to work isn't going to kill them. It'll probably save them. For starters, we live in a competitive society now, and your children are no longer competing against the neighborhood kids in their class. They're dealing with global competition in a marketplace in which whoever can get the job done efficiently and effectively can have it, no matter where they live in the world!

If the best a young adult has to offer is the same education most of their peers got, how competitive are they? Work experience, understanding hierarchy and corporate culture, the confidence of knowing how to interact with adults, and everything you learn from the responsibilities of a job will set those young people that work apart from those that don't. And at the end of the day, employers don't have time to help your children mature. They expect you to have already done that.

Here are a few work ideas for kids at different ages:

YOUNG KIDS: Younger children may not actually work in the traditional sense, but they can take on simple tasks around the home and garden to earn a little income. My five-year-old shreds paper in my home office or dusts windowsills throughout our home to earn money. When children get a little older, they can find odd jobs around the neighborhood, like mowing lawns, shoveling snow, weeding gardens, or raking leaves to earn a few extra bucks.

PRE-TEENS: During the pre-teen years, your children can earn their own cash by baby-sitting, pet-sitting, or tutoring other kids. This is a good time to teach them a little about entrepreneurship. Have them assess their gifts, talents, and likes to see if they could be the solution to any problems in the neighborhood.

TEENAGERS: Once your children reach the teenage years and show some financial maturity, you should encourage them to get part-time jobs. Teenagers can find work at supermarkets, restaurants, department stores, and other local businesses around your neighborhood. You'll ideally want something in walking distance, so they aren't stressing you about needing a car.

The opportunity to get a job needs to be accompanied by some rules. Not only should you help your teenager predetermine how earnings should be divvied up, so he or she understands your expectation for savings, you should also set other ground rules. Before agreeing to a particular job, discuss work hours, schoolwork commitments, expectations for grades, and household responsibilities with your teen.

WHAT SHOULD I BE DOING TO MAKE SURE
MY CHILD CAN ATTEND COLLEGE DEBT-FREE?

In its most recent survey of college pricing, the College Board reports that a "moderate" college budget for an in-state public college during the 2012–2013 academic year averaged $22,261. A moderate budget at a private college averaged $43,289. Now consider an additional independent 2012 study reporting 53% of recent college graduates are either unemployed or working as sales clerks, waiters, janitors, and other positions that don't require a college degree. While that's not what you want to hear as a parent, it's a reality you have to face. These are sobering statistics that should make you think twice about borrowing money for your kids to go to college, especially if you haven't saved at all or haven't saved enough for your own retirement.

UN REAL

In 2012, 53% of recent college graduates were unemployed or working in jobs that don't require a college degree.

Taking on a boatload of debt so your children don't have to be saddled with it isn't a good plan, but there are ways you can prepare for your children to go to college debt-free. You may be surprised to hear, however, that only a small portion of this plan will actually include you. Most of the work will be up to your children. Think less about what you have to do and more about how you'll teach them the importance of what *they* have to do.

For your part, one of the best things you can do is to save in a vehicle that's specifically set up for college expenses. If you think putting money aside in a regular savings account is going to do the trick, you should probably think again.

Real MONEY

It takes years of deliberate planning to create a debt-free strategy for attending college.

Look into a 529 plan. It's an account designed to encourage families to save for educational costs. It's almost like a 401k, except it's geared solely toward college expenses. A 529 comes in two forms: pre-paid and college savings.

The pre-paid plan allows you to purchase tuition credits in your state's university system at current tuition rates, which protects you against hikes in tuition. The potential downside is that your child may not get into a state school or may not be interested in attending one. In that case, you can withdraw the money and pay the penalties or transfer the plan to another child.

The college savings plan is a tax-advantaged account that allows you to accumulate assets to use toward any accredited college or vocational school in the United States. The funds can be used to pay for expenses like tuition costs, textbooks, and other education-related fees.

This going to college debt-free stuff is pretty much out of your hands from here. It takes years of deliberate planning to create a debt-free strategy for attending college.

Of course, you can harass and nag your kids, their teachers, and school administrators to death, but this works out so much better when you instill these two guiding principles in your child.

1. College is expensive.

2. You probably won't go unless you do your part.

Harsh? Yes. But for many, it's the reality, and they shouldn't be protected from the truth. It's not the kind of surprise anyone wants to get during the application process. It takes years of deliberate planning to create a debt-free strategy for attending college. Even the parents who dedicate their lives to little league sports to try to snag athletic scholarships understand that. Similarly, those of us with children who may not be athletically inclined need to put the same energy into creating a "scholarship brand" for our children as early as possible. Jessica Johnson, the founder of The Scholarship Academy, a non-profit organization that helps families create and perfect their scholarship brand, says children as young as second grade can begin not only creating their brand, but applying for scholarships.

The most important thing, Johnson says, is figuring out the child's likes and strengths and then making sure everything from extracurricular activities to volunteer opportunities support the same themes. Your child can look like an expert by eighteen and become a real asset to the right college program.

While The Scholarship Academy and programs like it focus on helping young people with average grades succeed in landing scholarships, a major factor in helping your kids go to college debt-free is encouraging them to keep their grades up, which is also ultimately their responsibility. Being awarded free money is really a numbers game. The better the student's grades are, the more opportunities he or she has to earn money neither of you will ever have to repay.

Some people are discouraged because of the smaller dollar amounts that many grants or scholarships offer, however it's important to realize that every dollar counts and can add up quickly. Any amount you don't have to borrow is an even larger amount you won't have to stress about paying back in the future. Seek out a resource at your child's school to help you navigate the financial aid process, and check out sites like www.scholarships.com.

Of course, you understand the importance of attending college debt-free, but that won't mean a hill of beans if they don't understand it, too.

HOW CAN I SAY *NO* TO MY ADULT CHILD?

Turning down other people who ask for money might be a cinch, but how the heck do you say *no* when it's your adult child? Many parents don't talk to young children about money because of the fear that the children will be burdened with adult worries before their time. There are two

AFFIRM

I empower others to create their own wealth and power.

holes in that theory. First, children won't fear something they fully understand. Education begets empowerment; ignorance does not. Second, little kids become big kids very quickly, and big kids become adults in the blink of an eye. If you miss this very small window of opportunity to teach your child the meaning of the word *no*, it's likely you'll have to continuously face these types of issues with your grown son or daughter.

The most important thing in these scenarios is to realize that while you may still see your cute little baby when you look at this person, your child has become an adult. This is an able-bodied person that you're both enabling and handicapping. This is a talented and gifted adult that you're hurting, not helping. Contrary to what you believe, your child can and will figure something out when you're not there to save her or him from the trials every adult may experience at some point in life.

Think about it. Have you experienced certain setbacks? Did you live to tell the story? Well, they will, too. Some of life's greatest lessons are learned through hard experiences. To appreciate the high moments in life, you have to know what the low points feel like. If you constantly shield your adult children from having to find a way back from those low points, you not only rob them of the satisfaction of knowing they can make it on their own, you block their chances to succeed and continuously make yourself out as the answer to all their problems. Once you're gone, they're left defenseless in the real world, which isn't what you want for them. Your goal should be to guide and empower them while they have you here.

The bottom line is to truly help someone, even your own child, you sometimes have to stop helping them. (See: *How do I find the courage to say "no" to a loved one that needs help?*)

VISIT MINDSETANDMONEYMASTERCLASS.COM

Are you finally ready to take your money mindset and skill set to the next level?

Take the Mindset + Money Master Class Today!

If you are sick and tired of being sick and tired and know you deserve better, can DO better and are READY TO discover your purpose, truly profit on your gift and achieve the personal finance success you desire, then this is the class you've been searching for!

- ☑ *Get clear about your purpose and how that contributes to financial success.*

- ☑ *Create a plan to put at least $500 of extra CASH in your pocket FAST!*

- ☑ *Discover an easy method for determining your DEBT-FREE date and what you can do to cut it in HALF!*

- ☑ *Techniques for conquering the fear & anxiety you experience when its time to tell a loved one, "NO!"*

- ☑ *And Much, Much More!*

Stop settling for financial stress.
Its time to get financial strategies
you can use immediately!

**Visit MindsetAndMoneyMasterClass.com
for more details!**

MINDSET + MONEY
M A S T E R   C L A S S
with
PATRICE C. WASHINGTON

APPENDIX A
PRINT RESOURCES

THE FOLLOWING BOOKS MAY prove to be excellent resources for developing further knowledge around what you have learned in *Real Money Answers for Men*. My hope is that by browsing through the resources below you will ultimately find the style that works best for you. Your journey cannot stop with Real Money Answers. This book is a tool to assist you with becoming aware about how to make healthy financial decisions. Additional resources will ensure that you maintain them as you move through your money journey and quest for financial freedom. Enjoy!

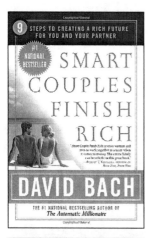

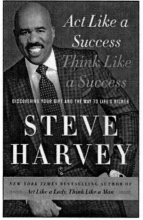

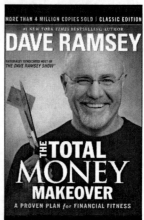

APPENDIX B
SAMPLE LETTERS

CREDIT REPORT DISPUTE LETTER

Debt B. Gone
123 Your Home Address
Your Town, GA 01234

The Credit Bureau
Bureau Address
Anytown, ST 56789

Date

Dear Credit Bureau,

This letter is a formal complaint that you are reporting inaccurate credit information. I am very distressed that you have included the below information in my credit profile due to its damaging effects on my good credit standing. As you are aware, credit reporting laws ensure that bureaus report only accurate credit information. No doubt the inclusion of this inaccurate information is a mistake on either your or the reporting creditor's part. Because of the mistakes on my credit report, I have been wrongfully denied credit recently for a <insert credit type for which you were denied here>, which was highly embarrassing and has negatively impacted my lifestyle. The following information therefore needs to be verified and deleted from the report as soon as possible: CREDITOR AGENCY, acct. 123-34567-ABC Please delete the above information as quickly as possible.

Sincerely,
Signature
Printed Name
SSN# 123-45-6789

Attachment included.

(Don't forget to provide proof if you have it! Keep a copy for your files and send the letter registered mail.)

* Remember this can also be done online by visiting the credit bureaus website.

DISPUTE LETTER TO INDIVIDUAL CREDITOR

Date
Company name
Address

Re: Acct # XXXX-XXXX-XXXX-XXXX

Dear CEO name,

I am writing to you today regarding my credit card account #4236-XXXX-XXXX-XXXX which I had while I was a student at ------------------------. The purpose of my correspondence is to see if you would be willing to make a "goodwill" adjustment on the reporting of this account to the three credit agencies.

During the time period this account was established I had was very happy with the service, I was however not the ideal customer and made mistakes with my handling of the account. I should have kept better records regarding the account and I take full responsibility. I became aware of the unpaid balance when I got a copy of my credit report in _____ of 20____.

I know that payment was my responsibility. I am not attempting to justify this breach of my user agreement. I was, however, hoping you might review the circumstances under which this non-payment occurred and consider removing the negative trade line from my credit reports.

As soon as I became aware of the balance I contacted ---------------- and paid the balance in full. I provide this not to justify why the account was unpaid, but rather to show that the issue with ----------- is not a good indicator of my actual credit worthiness. I hope that ---------------- is willing to work with me on erasing this mark from my credit reports.

I would like to STRESS that the information currently being reported IS accurate, (I am not disputing anything with ---------------). I am simply asking ------------for a courtesy gesture of goodwill in having the credit bureaus remove this account from my report. I do recognize that this request is unique and that it may not be ------------ normal policy. Please consider that the Fair Credit Reporting Act does not demand that all accounts be reported, only that any account that is reported be reported accurately. Therefore, a company does have legal discretion and permission to remove any account it chooses from the credit report. I'm hoping that ------------ will do that in my case for this account.

Your kind consideration in this matter is greatly appreciated.

Best Regards
Signature
Printed Name

LETTER TO HARASSING CREDITOR

Sally B. Struggle
123 Your Home Address
Your Home Town, CA 01234

Harassing Creditor
Creditor Address
Anytown, ST 56789

RE: Account Number

Date

Dear Harassing Creditor,

To whom it may concern:

Please be advised that on the following dates, _____, I requested that your representative _____ stop calling me at home or at work. These continuous calls are serving no purpose but to harass me. I realize that I have a financial obligation to your company. However, my present financial situation makes it impossible for me to meet our original terms.
I am exercising my right granted by the Bureau of Consumer Protection, a division of the Federal
Trade Commission, to request that no one from your company call me at home or at work again.

If you must contact me, please do it via U.S. Postal Service.

Thank you in advance for your cooperation.

Sincerely,
Signature
Printed Name

APPENDIX C
ASSORTED WORKSHEETS

CREATING A PERSONAL FINANCIAL PLAN

These questions are the foundation for creating a personal financial plan.

1. Assessment: *Where are you now*? Use numbers and dollar amounts to be specific about where you are with respect to savings, debt and any other financial data you want to start tracking.

_____

_____

_____

_____

_____

2. Goal Setting: *Where do you want to be?* Again use specific terms to define where you would like to be financially by a set time at some point in the near future.

_____

_____

_____

_____

_____

3. Creating a Plan: *How will you get there?* Do you need to stop spending or get a job in order to reach your goals? List three things you can begin doing within the next 30 days to get you on track.

_____

_____

_____

_____

_____

4. Execution: *Taking action and making it happen.* There's no time like the present to take action on creating the life you say you want! List an action you can start in the next 24 hours.

_____

_____

_____

_____

_____

5. Re-Assessment: *Repeating the process regularly.* Determine in advance how often throughout the year you will check in on your progress and re-assess if necessary. I would suggest at least every six months.

_____

_____

_____

_____

_____

SAMPLE MONTHLY BUDGET

Of course your expenses and therefore, budget, will vary based on your personal lifestyle habits, but this is a great place to begin to list the numbers you'll need to work with. Remember, it doesn't matter which budget you use – you just need to use something!

PATRICE WASHINGTON
Author | Speaker | Coach

MONTHLY PROSPERITY PLAN

Monthly Income		Monthly Expenses	
Your Pay	$	Rent or Mortgage	$
Spouse's Pay	$	Utilities (Phone, gas, electric, cable, etc.)	$
Bonuses	$	Insurance (home, auto, life, health, etc.)	$
Commissions	$	Food	$
Tips	$	Incidental Home (non-food Items, etc.)	$
Interest Received	$	Clothing	$
Investment Earnings	$	Auto (car note, gas, maintenance)	$
Rental Income	$	Debt Payments (credit cards, store cards, etc.)	$
Pension Income	$	Child Care	$
Social Security Income	$	Health (medical, dental, eye, etc./not covered)	$
Alimony Received	$	Taxes (not taken out of paycheck)	$
Child Support Received	$	Gifts (charities, church)	$
Other Income	$	Entertainment (movies, vacation, videos, etc.)	$
	$	Personal Allowances	$
	$	Other Expenses	$
	$		$
Totals	$		$

MEET PATRICE C. WASHINGTON

Patrice C. Washington has been making learning about money a fun and exciting experience since 2003. She is a best-selling author, national personal finance speaker, and the Money Maven of her own weekly "Real Money Answers" segment on the nationally syndicated *Steve Harvey Morning Show*, empowering millions to take control of their finances.

Patrice's wisdom on money matters has been featured by national brands including NBC, *The Huffington Post* and *Black Enterprise*.

Each year, conferences, churches, and colleges from coast to coast engage Patrice to entertain, empower, and educate thousands of people about personal finance, career advancement, entrepreneurship, and success. Patrice doesn't bore audiences with financial jargon and fluff they can't use. She candidly tells the story of her own journey because, unlike many experts, she wants you to learn as much from her mistakes and setbacks as you do from her triumphs. After writing hundreds articles for print and online media, Patrice has become the go-to expert for practical money tips you can implement immediately.

When Patrice isn't making audiences laugh and learn somewhere around the country, she's at home in Atlanta, Georgia, being entertained by her fun-loving daughter, Reagan, and extremely supportive husband, Gerald.

For more about Patrice, visit www.BookTheMoneyMaven.com.

CPSIA information can be obtained at www.ICGtesting.com
Printed in the USA
LVOW08s2251291215

468355LV00014B/508/P